Design

The Kriegsmarine commissioned 40 destroyers between January 1937 and March 1944 and all saw service in World War II; 25 were lost. Designed for the Baltic and North Sea, their wartime area of operations stretched from the Gulf of Finland to the North Cape of Norway and to Cape Finisterre in Spain. Modern, fast, large, and heavily armed, they were potentially formidable adversaries but ultimately their effectiveness was limited due to unreliable machinery and poor seakeeping qualities.

The Treaty of Versailles limited the German Navy to 16 destroyers and 16 torpedo boats, but only 12 of each could be in commission at any one time. The destroyers dated from 1910 to 1913 and could be replaced when they reached 15 years of age; replacements could not displace more than 600 tons. Economic instability and political upheaval in Germany prevented any work on replacement destroyers until November 1932 when the Reichsmarine rebuilding plan was approved.

The basic specifications stipulated high speed and heavy armament: high speed for offensive minelaying and to screen the projected *Scharnhorst* class battlecruisers with their 33kt top speed; heavy armament to match new designs from the most likely adversaries, France and Poland.

In response to invitations, sketch designs were submitted by Stettin Vulcan for a ship of 1100 tons capable of 35kts carrying three 5in guns and six 21in torpedo tubes, and by Schichau for a ship of 1500 tons capable of 38kts and carrying four 5in guns and six 21in torpedo tubes. The 1500-ton design was selected as the basis for detailed design work, which was done in secret as the displacement considerably exceeded the provisions of the Treaty of Versailles.

In May 1933, in anticipation of Germany tearing up the Treaty of Versailles and becoming a signatory to the London Naval Treaty which allowed destroyers up to 1850 tons, Reichsmarine chief Admiral Raeder increased the displacement to 1850 tons with five 5in guns and eight 21in torpedo tubes.

The design was rushed and decisions were made regarding hull shape, machinery, and armament that would later manifest themselves as serious weaknesses. Not surprisingly, as the first German destroyers built since 1918, the final design closely resembled the *S113/V116* of 1918 with two tall funnels, straight bows, no sheer, a raised turtleback

Z1 Leberecht Maass as built with rounded upper bridge, straight stem, and bridge eagle. The tops of the binocular sight, rangefinder, and TAM (a target rate of change of bearing instrument) can be seen atop the bridge under their canvas covers. Just in front of the amidships cutter the twin 37mm is similarly covered. *(Author's collection)*

forecastle, and hull with a slight tumblehome from the forecastle break to the stern. The main armament was in single shielded mounts, two forward and three aft. Two quadruple torpedo tube mounts were carried on the centreline, one forward and one aft of the after funnel.

The basic design was now set for all 40 German built destroyers that would see action in World War II. While there would be six different classes (three with 5.9in guns), the hull shape, internal arrangements, armament layout, and power plant were effectively the same for all. At over 2200 tons standard displacement, they were nearly twice the size of the Royal Navy's 'G' class, but equivalent to the larger French *Mogador*, *L'Audacieux*, and *2400-tonne* classes.

Orders were confirmed on 1 April 1934 and the first four ships were contracted to the government yard of Deutche Werke at Kiel.

Hull and Superstructure. The hull was of all-welded construction, and there were fifteen watertight compartments numbered from stern to bow, the aftermost being No 1 and the foremost No 15. The machinery spaces were in compartments 4 to 10, taking up nearly half of the hull length. From the stern, they comprised Turbine Room No 1, an auxiliary machinery room, Turbine Room No 2, Boiler Room No 1, the diesel generator and auxiliary boiler room, Boiler Room No 2, and Boiler Room No 3. The port propeller shaft was powered from Turbine Room 1, the starboard from Turbine Room 2. Boiler Room 1 vented through the after funnel, Boiler Rooms 2 and 3 vented through the forward funnel.

Crew accommodation, officer's cabins, and magazine spaces took up the rest of the hull compartments. Fuel oil was carried in tanks outboard of the machinery spaces. The double bottom below the machinery spaces contained additional fuel bunkers, lubricating oil tanks, and boiler feed water.

All decks were steel plate. The exposed decks carried a welded-on raised pattern for grip, which was not very effective in rough

DESIGN PARTICULARS

Displacement (tons)

Type 1934:	2223 standard, 3156 full load
Type 1934A:	*Z5–Z8* 2171 standard, 3110 full load; *Z9–Z13* 2270 standard, 3190 full load; *Z14–Z16* 2239 standard, 3165 full load
Type 1936:	2411 standard, 3415 full load
Type 1936A:	*Z23–Z24* 2603 standard, 3605 full load; *Z25–Z27* 3079 standard, 3543 full load; *Z28* 2596 standard, 3519 full load; *Z29–Z30* 2603 standard, 3597 full load
Type 1936A (Mob):	2757 standard, 3691 full load
Type 1936B (Mob):	2519 standard, 3542 full load

Length (feet)

Type 1934 & 1934A:	374 pp, 381.2 wl, 390.4 oa
Type 1936:	374 pp, 382.2 pp, 404.8 (*Z20–Z22* 410.4) oa
Type 1936A, 1936A (Mob):	374 pp, 400 wl, 416.6 oa
Type 1936B (Mob):	374 pp, 398.6 wl, 416.6 oa

Beam (feet)

Type 1934 & 1934A:	37.0. Type 1936: 38.5. Type 1936A, 1936A (Mob) & 1936B (Mob): 39.3

Draught (max, feet)

Type 1934 & 1934A:	13.8. Type 1936: 14.7. Type 1936A: 15.2 (*Z25–Z27* 14.5; *Z28* 14.3; *Z29–Z30* 15.1). Type 1936A (Mob): 15.1. Type 1936B (Mob):14.1

Machinery

All Types:	6 Wagner 1028psi (except *Z9–Z16* 6 Benson 1616psi) boilers, 2 Wagner geared turbines; 70,000shp; speed 38 (except Type 1936A and later 36–38) knots

Fuel (tons)/range @ 19 knots

Type 1934 & 1934A:	770/1900nm (*Z9–Z16* 670/1530nm)
Type 1936:	787/2020nm
Type 1936A:	801/2174nm (*Z28* 769/2087nm, *Z29–Z30* 825/2239nm)
Type 1936A (Mob):	835/2239nm
Type 1936B (Mob):	825/2950nm

Armament

Types 1934, 1934A, 1936:	5x1 5in SK C/34 120rpg; 2x2 37mm SK C/30 2000rpg; 6x1 20mm C/30 2000rpg; 2x4 21in torpedo tubes; 60 mines
Type 1936A:	1x2 5.9in TBK C/36 120rpg; 3x1 5.9in TBK C/36 120rpg (except *Z28* 4x1 5.9in TBK C/36 120rpg); 2x2 37mm SK C/30 2000rpg; 6 x1 20mm C/30 2000rpg; 2x4 21in torpedo tubes; 60 mines
Type 1936A (Mob):	As Type 1936A, plus 1x4 20mm C/30 2000rpg
Type 1936B (Mob):	5x1 5in SK C/34 120rpg; 2x2 37mm SK C/30 2000rpg; 3x4 20mm C/30 2000rpg: 2x2 20mm C/30 2000rpg; 2x4 21in torpedo tubes; 76 mines

Complement (+ extra as flagship)

Type 1934, 1934, Type 1936 & *Z28*: 323–327 + 23; Type 1936A: 336 + 23; Type 1936A (Mob): 336 + 23; Type 1936B (Mob): 336

water; non-slip paint or compounds were not used. The bridge decks were covered with wood. The bridge structure contained the wheelhouse, radio and coding offices, captain's sea cabin, chart room, and ammunition handling room. The after deckhouse contained the wardroom, captain's quarters with sleeping cabin, bath, heads and pantry. Two searchlights were fitted: one on the foremast and one behind the after funnel.

The underwater hull contained some interesting design features. It was optimised for high speed with very fine lines forward and a transom stern aft. A downward sloping deflector wedge (*'staukeil'*) was fitted aft of the propellers to push the propeller wash downwards and raise the stern, keeping the ship level at high speeds to improve seakeeping. A skeg on the centerline reduced lateral movement. These design features would all prove disastrous.

Machinery. The mechanical energy derived from steam is a function of steam temperature; the higher the temperature, the more mechanical energy. Increasing the operating pressure of the boiler is one way to increase steam temperature. Boilers that operate at higher pressures offer several advantages over lower pressure boilers: they are more compact, use less fuel, and come to working temperature quicker. Understandably, the Kriegsmarine took a great interest in the tactical advantages of these features.

An experimental high-pressure system which operated at 330psi and 450°C had been installed and operated successfully aboard the freighter *Uckermark*; the fuel

Z2 George Thiele after 1938 refit with raised forecastle and enlarged bridge. Both searchlight platforms and the top of the after deckhouse are enclosed with canvas screens. Note the dinghy stowed on its side under the AA deck and the position of the TAM directly under the forward searchlight. Funnel cowls are silver. *(Author's collection)*

Z5 Paul Jacobi as built with rounded upper bridge. The bridge fire control instruments are not covered and the rangefinders are trained to port – the after searchlight is not fitted. Note the amount of spray forward and aft. Funnel cowls are silver.

Z9 Wolfgang Zenker as built with raked bow. There are canvas screens fitted around the after deckhouse roof, the after gun deck, and the AA deck. Note the boiler intake vents at the bottom of both funnels, the dinghy under the AA deck, and the control positions atop the torpedo tubes. The two-tone colour scheme is quite evident; funnel cowls are silver. *(Author's collection)*

savings were estimated at 50 per cent over a conventional steam power plant. While there was much back and forth in the design department regarding the proposed power plant, ultimately the high-pressure system was selected. The Kriegsmarine did not get involved in system design, leaving that to the manufacturers who preferred to use theoretical concepts instead of engaging in practical research. Automatic control of combustion was a required design feature and a complicated arrangement of jets, servos, bellows, and cams was used to regulate fuel quantity and air pressure.

Two boiler designs were selected for installation: the Wagner boiler had natural water circulation and operated at 1028psi and 450°C; the Benson boiler had forced feed circulation and operated at 1616psi and 510°C. *Z9–Z16* were fitted with Benson boilers, the rest with Wagner's. Six boilers generating a total of 70,000 SHP were fitted to each ship, two per boiler room.

By way of comparison, the Royal Navy Admiralty boilers of the time operated at 200psi and 316°C; an increase to 500psi and 325°C was felt too much of an advance. The experimental Japanese destroyer *Shimakaze* of 1943 operated at 571psi and 400°C. Clearly the German navy was on the very leading edge of boiler technology.

The ships could attain 27kts on just two boilers and 32kts on four. The time to raise steam was short, as illustrated on 17 October 1940 when it took nine minutes to get the turbines up to full power after lighting off two cold boilers on one of the destroyers being pursued by British forces in the South Western Approaches.

Testing was done at the yards, but this was terminated in summer 1934 and trials began aboard the yacht *Grille*, escorts *F1* to *F10* and the training ship *Brummer*. The trial results were of little practical value as there was no time or inclination to make changes to the power plants already being fitted to the destroyers. The inevitable teething problems and development of standard operating procedures were left to the engineering staffs aboard the ships themselves.

Z1–Z4 were fitted with cruising turbines, but the remainder were not, due to problems with the clutching arrangement. From the Type 1936A onwards, material supply problems led to the propeller shaft bearings being made from synthetic plastic rather than the usual white metal, and much of the piping was steel instead of non-ferrous metals such as aluminum, copper, zinc, or brass alloy.

Unfortunately, the decision to install high-pressure steam plants would also prove disastrous.

Electrical power. Main electrical power came from two 200kw turbo generators, one in each turbine room. Diesel generators took over the load when boilers were shut down. As a comparison, the RN 'Tribal' class produced a total of 190kw, suggesting that a lot of auxiliary equipment in the German ships was power assisted.

Anti-roll system. *Z1–Z22* were fitted with an electric anti-roll system which used two trim tanks amidships. The system was not a success and it was removed and replaced with bilge keels. *Z20* retained the system for experimental purposes.

Main gun armament. Twenty-five of the destroyers were fitted with the 5in gun mounted singly in open backed armoured shields. It was a low-angle gun suitable for engaging surface targets only; while it had no inherent high-angle anti-aircraft capability it was used for low-angle long range barrage fire against low flying aircraft. Five mounts were fitted, two forward and three aft, numbered sequentially from forward, No 1 being the foremost and No 5 the aftermost. All had considerable arcs of fire except for No 3 amidships which was restricted to 30° forward and 150° aft of the beam.

The ammunition supply hoists were electrically powered; 120 rounds per gun were carried. As a well-practiced crew could achieve a rate of fire of 15–18 rounds per minute, the entire supply could be expended within eight minutes, which is why most of the destroyers in the Narvik battles in 1940 ran out of ammunition. In contrast, the Royal Navy 'G' class carried 200 rounds per gun for the 4.7in and this was considered enough for 35 minutes' action.

In an attempt to provide the firepower of a light cruiser on a destroyer hull, fifteen of the destroyers were fitted with the 5.9in gun. It was reasoned that the rate of fire would be very similar to that of the 5in, but would provide far greater hitting power at a longer effective range. The 5.9in gun was mounted either singly in open backed armoured shields, or as a twin in a fully enclosed lightweight armoured gunhouse/turret. Like the 5in, the gun was suitable for low-angle fire only, with no inherent anti-aircraft capability. The twin guns fitted in the turret could elevate to 65°, but a lack of a high angle director and the low rate of fire hampered its use in the AA role. Both types of mounting were capable of AA barrage fire against low flying aircraft.

Four mounts were fitted, one forward and three aft, again numbered sequentially from forward; the forward mount was either a single or the twin turret. The firing arcs of No 2 mount amidships were restricted. *Z28* was fitted with two single mounts forward and two aft as she was configured as a flotilla leader with an enlarged after deckhouse. The turret provided shelter for the crews and concentrated the firepower of two single mounts. It used electric power for training and hydraulics for elevation, the two guns were in the same sleeve and could not elevate separately.

The prototype 5.9in single mounts were fitted and tested aboard *Z8* when she was completed. The tests were carried out in relatively benign conditions in the Baltic and at their conclusion the go-ahead was given to proceed with the production and fitting of the larger gun – another disastrous decision.

Following action damage in January 1945 which destroyed her forward turret, *Z31* was fitted with a single shielded 4.1in in its place which she carried until the end of the war.

Anti-aircraft armament. The light AA consisted of 37mm and 20mm guns. The 37mm C/30 was a stabilised twin mount, although it had difficulty tracking targets when the ship was making sharp turns and/or rolling. It was replaced with the far more effective 37mm Mk 42 which became available in 1944, fitted in either a single or twin mount.

The 20mm gun originally fitted was the C/30 which was prone to jamming; fitted with a 20-round magazine, it also required frequent stoppages to swap it out. It was replaced with the improved C/38 which had a 40-round magazine. The guns were mounted singly, as twins, or in a quad mount ('*vierling*'). A fully stabilised quad became available in 1944.

All of the AA guns were trained by the use of hand wheels; there was no power operation, nor were they free-swinging. Their effectiveness was hampered by handheld rangefinders and the lack of HA remote control. The 37mm guns were mounted on an AA Deck built around the after funnel. Starting with the Type 1936, this deck was

Z18 Hans Lüdemann showing several features of the Type 1936 – shorter and wider funnels, small propeller guards, mainmast atop the after deckhouse, cutter on shorter davits, and the TAM on the pedestal underneath the forward searchlight. Other items of interest are the covered depth charge throwers on the main deck under the after deckhouse and the name plate forward of the propeller guard; funnel cowls are silver. *(Author's collection)*

ARMAMENT CHARACTERISTICS

Weapon	Mounting Weight	Armour (inches)	Maximum Elevation	Horizontal Range (yards)	Vertical Range (feet)	Rate of fire (rpm)	Round Weight (lbs)
5.9in/48 C/36 single	17.7 tons	0.39 face 0.23 side	30	24,000	N/A	7-8	99.2 shell 51.8 charge
5.9in/48 C/36 twin turret	66.6 tons	1.18 face 0.78 side	65	24,000	N/A	7-8	99.2 shell 51.8 charge
5in/45 C/34	11.2 tons	0.31 face 0.31 side	30	19,000	N/A	15-18	61.7 shell 35.2 charge
4.1in/45 SK C/32	7.4 tons	0.47 face 0.15 side	70	16,595	N/A	15	33.2 shell 8.3 charge
37mm SK C/30	4.0 tons	N/A	85	9295	22,300	30	4.6
37mm Mk 42	1.3 tons	N/A	90	7000	15,740	250	2.8
20mm C/30	925 lbs	N/A	85	5350	12,130	120	0.7
20mm C/38	917 lbs	N/A	85	5350	12,130	220	0.7
20mm Flak 35 Quad	2.3 tons	N/A	85	5350	12,130	880	0.7

enlarged to accommodate 20mm mounts as well. Not all ships carried their full allotment of 20mm singles when completed

The RAG system of unguided surface-to-air missiles with an effective range of 5000yds was installed on several ships after mid-1944. It was similar to the UP projectile with trailing wires that would remain airborne for 20 seconds, allowing a barrage to be fired at attacking aircraft. The launchers were simple tubes and 28 rounds were stowed for each launcher in ready-use lockers.

Torpedoes. The torpedo tubes were in quadruple mounts fitted on the centreline casing above the machinery spaces; the two centre tubes were set slightly back from the outer tubes to prevent interference when a full salvo of four was fired. Each mount was fitted with an open control position with director sights and power training controls; the tubes could be also trained and fired from the bridge using remote power control. Weather shields of plexiglass or metal were fitted over the control positions on some ships.

Twelve torpedoes were carried; eight in the tubes and four reloads in compartments located in the raised casing that the torpedo mounts sat on, one compartment on each side of each mount. Starting with the Type 1936A, the reloads were stowed in metal lockers on the main deck. Heavy girders fitted at the front of the AA deck and at the front of the after superstructure could be swung out and fitted with a boom block and tackle arrangement to reload the tubes or to withdraw the torpedoes for maintenance. The torpedoes could also be placed on trolleys which ran on the mine rails. Unlike the Japanese dedicated reload gear, the system was cumbersome and not suited to battle conditions.

The torpedo was the standard G7A powered by compressed air and carrying a 600lb warhead. It could be set to run 13,000yds at 30kts, 8000yds at 40kts, or 4300yds at 45kts and could be gyro angled to turn up to 90° after launch.

Depth charges. There were two throwers on each side of the main deck abreast the after superstructure with two ready-use

Z20 Karl Galster with her original bridge configuration; the Atlantic bow is not readily apparent from this viewing angle. She is fitted with both searchlights but not a crowsnest. The forward searchlight is well above the fore funnel – it could be positioned on the foremast at several different heights from here down to just above the TAM. Note the port side cutter fitted to the Type 1936; funnel cowls are silver. Even at slow speed, the ship is trimmed down at the bow. *(Author's collection)*

The combination of the quad 20mm in front of the bridge and on the after deckhouse, the single 5.9in mount forward, and the weather shields on the torpedo tubes makes it most likely that this Type 1936A is *Z27*. Note the shortened bridge and positioning of the FuMO 21 to allow it to rotate. She is carrying life rafts on the gun mounts and bridge wings, and is not fitted with a tripod foremast.

Z31 in 1945 with the characteristic curved forward funnel cowl of the Type 1936A (Mob). Fitted with a single 4.1in gun forward, weather shields on the torpedo tubes, a FuMO 63 array in place of the after searchlight, and a degaussing cable. Just visible below the bridge are two of the forward twin 37mm mounts.

reloads stacked alongside. Only 18 depth charges were carried in total during peace time, but by the end of the war, *Z33* was equipped with a total of 30 depth charges.

Mines. Removable mine rails were fitted on both sides of the main deck. On the port side they ran from the forecastle break to the stern; on the starboard side they ran from the after funnel to the stern. The mines were fitted with wheeled sinkers and would be loaded directly onto the rails. To drop the mines, the crew would manually push them to the stern where they would drop off the mine rails. At the beginning of the war the mines were of two types: the EMC moored contact mine with a 660lb explosive charge and the EMF moored magnetic mine with a 770lb explosive charge.

Fire control. At the front of the upper bridge was a stabilized binocular sight with no weather protection which served as the main armament director. Immediately behind was a 13ft optical stereoscopic rangefinder for the forward guns. A rate of change of bearing instrument ('TAM') was at the rear of the bridge. Torpedo directors (stabilized from the Type 1936A onwards) were in the bridge wings; a second 13ft optical rangefinder was fitted behind the after funnel for the after guns. The main director and both rangefinders were linked to a central fire control transmitting station located under the bridge which determined gunnery solutions. No high angle capability was available. Torpedo firing solutions were determined by calculator boxes attached to the torpedo directors. The directors provided the target bearing, the TAM the rate of change of bearing, the optical rangefinders the range. The central fire control transmitting station could be used to determine a firing solution if time permitted. The control positons on the top of the tubes had a binocular sight with a calculator box. Both the 37mm and 20mm were served by handheld rangefinders.

Sensors. The Type GHG hydrophone system was the submarine detection device fitted to the pre-war Type 1934, 1934A, and 1936 classes. It consisted of 36 receivers built into each side of the hull and operated passively; the operators had to listen for submarine noises. Range varied considerably according to ocean conditions, but a

A Type 1936A or Type 1936A (Mob) with No.2 gun, rangefinder, and searchlight bearing to starboard. There is a twin 37mm and a single 20mm on the AA deck; note the life rafts stowed on the platform immediately behind the AA deck and against the back of the bridge wing. The ship is fitted with a cutter on the starboard side forward. The large girder in the lower foreground is for hoisting reload torpedoes.

Z28 as built with her large after deckhouse with mainmast at the rear and two single 20mm at the forward end. Life rafts are fitted to the gun mounts and against the bridge wings; a single 20mm is on the forecastle. Her radar set has not yet been fitted.

Amidships detail aboard a Type 1936A destroyer. Items of interest include the square exhaust vent fitted to the forward funnel, life rafts behind the forward funnel, lifelines, depth charge throwers, canvas screens on the AA deck with a life raft on the front, a ship's boat across the front of the torpedo tubes, and a camouflage pattern on the after funnel. The ship is not carrying a reload torpedo locker nor the reload gear on the starboard side.

submarine proceeding at full speed could be heard from 550–760yds. The S-Gerät echo-ranging system with a protruding underwater dome was developed in the 1930s. It was installed in the pre-war destroyers beginning in 1940; the later classes probably completed with the equipment.

Beginning with the Type 1936A, the destroyers were fitted with active search radar (designated FuMO or FuMZ) and passive radar detectors (designated FuMB); the equipment was fitted to the earlier ships as they came in for refit.

There were many different varieties of each type. Many were experimental and only fitted to a few ships near the end of the war. These were the principal sets:

FuMO 21 was a 6.5ft x 13ft mattress and was fitted to the top of the radar office at the back of the bridge. This unit was not fully trainable on the earlier ships due to the close proximity of the foremast.

FuMO 24/25 was an improved and larger mattress 6.5ft x 20ft and was fitted to the top of the radar office. Some of the earlier ships had their foremast altered to a goalpost shape (*'tormast'*) to allow the unit to rotate.

FuMO 63 was a smaller mattress and was fitted in place of the after searchlight or on the foremast.

The passive radar detectors were in the form of aerials fitted to the foremast; the principal unit was the FuMB Metox. There was also an IFF aerial, the FuME 2 Wespe.

CAPTURED DESTROYERS

The Dutch destroyer *Gerard Callenburgh* was found scuttled at Rotterdam after the invasion of Holland in May 1940. Raised and commissioned into the German navy as *ZH1*, her completion was much delayed by sabotage in the Dutch yards.

The Greek destroyer *Vasilefs Georgios* was scuttled in a floating dock at Salamis in April 1941 while undergoing repairs. After being raised and repaired she was commissioned into the Kriegsmarine as *ZG3* and given the name *Hermes*. She spent her entire career in the Mediterranean.

PROJECTED TYPES

The Kriegsmarine design department continued to churn out design studies as the war progressed. Only two designs progressed beyond the drawing board.

Type 1936C. This was a modification of the

Crew members enjoying some spare time aboard a Type 1936A or Type 1936A (Mob) destroyer. The sighting ports are open on both gun mounts; note how the two different sizes of life rafts are attached. Other items of interest are the quad 20mm atop the after deckhouse, the mine rails, and the mesh on the railings on the after gun deck.

Type 1936A fitted with three twin 5in DP guns, one forward and two aft and fitted with radar controlled fire direction. Five were ordered; *Z46* and *Z47* were laid down at Deschimag in April 1943, but neither was launched and both were damaged in air raids while still on the stocks.

Type 1942. Another modification of the Type 1936A, this design was diesel powered and fitted with four single 5in DP mounts and six torpedo tubes. To get the required horsepower to reach 36kts, four MAN diesels driving three shafts were required. Endurance was predicted to be 11,000nm under operational conditions. *Z51* was ordered as a prototype in November 1942 and was launched in 1944, but was sunk in an air raid at Bremen while fitting out on 21 March 1945.

CRITICISM OF THE DESIGN

Hull. There were two problems with the underwater hull: the fine hull lines forward resulted in a relative lack of buoyancy at the bows and the stern deflector wedge which raised the stern but pushed the bows downwards in response. These two features in combination with the lack of sheer and flare in the bow section resulted in the bow digging into oncoming waves instead of riding over them, bringing seas aboard and throwing spray over the bridge in anything except calm conditions. In heavy seas, the effect made the forward gun mounts totally unworkable.

After digging in, the bows would eventually lift but the stern wedge would still be acting to raise the stern. With both ends of the ship moving upwards, the result was a permanent hull sagging problem amidships. Hull and deck cracks developed which required stiffening plates to be added. Along the bottom of the hull, the hull sagging opened weld lines in the double bottom fuel and feed water tanks, allowing in salt water which eventually found its way into the machinery and caused failures there. At the stern, the combination of the wedge and centreline skeg created a tunnel effect around the propellers which caused turbulence, leading to cavitation and loss of propeller and rudder efficiency.

Overall stability was effected by the fine underwater lines, the heavy superstructure, heavy armament, and the fuel stored outboard of the machinery spaces. Fuel in the tanks would tend to accumulate on the low side of any heel, greatly exaggerating any roll and resisting a return to upright. To make matters worse, the double bottom fuel tanks had to be emptied into the outboard tanks in order to be used, so as fuel levels dropped there would be less weight at the bottom of the hull.

The overall effect of these issues produced ships that rolled heavily and were frequently awash, making them poor gunnery platforms. While none of the ships capsized (rolls of up to 50° were experienced during the invasion of Norway), open ocean operations were frequently compromised by their poor seakeeping qualities. The problems caused by the stern wedge were recognised and starting with the Type 1936, it was reduced in size. The underwater hull shape was never changed; the ships still dug in their bows despite the fitting of the Atlantic bow from *Z20* onwards.

Machinery. The theoretical benefits of high pressure steam were not realised in practice due to a litany of faults. Both boiler types suffered continual boiler and super-heater

Z38 in 1943 in overall dark grey fitted with a degaussing cable, short spray strake forward, and both searchlights; funnel cowls are silver. The lighter patches on the bridge are probably her tactical number boards, covered up in this view. Note the clean entry of the bow compared to the earlier Type 1934/34A ships.

tube failures as a combination of poor workmanship, poor quality control, the tortuous curves required for natural circulation in the Wagner, poor circulation in the Benson, corrosion caused by the inability to fully drain the boiler tubes for maintenance, and tube alloys which could not withstand the high temperatures and pressures.

Valves, joints, seals, and packing were constant sources of failure, mainly due to the high pressures involved. The condensers were prone to breakdown, oil and lubrication lines also frequently leaked. Salt deposits in the super-heaters were common, especially with the Benson boilers which could only be cleaned with chemicals. Salt water frequently found its way into the fuel and feed water due to leaks in the double bottom tanks. There was no reserve feed water, so leaks anywhere in the feed water supply system could quickly cause a boiler shutdown and reduce range to a few hundred miles.

The boiler auxiliary equipment, such as pumps and preheaters, was all steam powered, which was an enormous drain on the steam made available for the turbines; the Benson boilers had over thirty pieces of auxiliary gear. Even when alongside, much of the auxiliary gear required power so boilers had to be kept fired, wasting fuel and affecting maintenance cycles. Placing two boilers in each boiler room along with all their auxiliary equipment resulted in very cramped machinery spaces with some of the equipment being almost inaccessible at sea. This meant the ships had to be docked for even minor repair.

When the automatic control system failed or did not respond quickly enough, manual control of the boilers was required. The complement of one NCO and four ratings per boiler was insufficient for effective manual control, seven being the minimum number required. Adding engine room crew members was not possible as there was not enough accommodation space.

Leakages, split tubes, and fires had to be overcome on every voyage. The builders themselves were operating at the limit of their experience and did not have much practical advice or training to offer. The Engineering Director at Germania-Werft told *Z13*'s chief engineer that while he knew how the installation worked, he had no confidence that he could get it to work at

Z39 as completed in August 1943 sporting her unique spray strake/degaussing cable encircling the hull at main deck level. The quad 20mm in front of the bridge and one of the twin 37mm on the AA deck can be seen; the radar array is FuMO 21. The distinguishing features of the Type 1936A (Mob) are clearly evident: squared off bridge wings, starboard side forecastle derrick, and curve to the forward funnel cap. Funnel cowls are silver.

Z4 Richard Beitzen off Brittany in 1940 in a photo that graphically shows how the Type 1934 ships drove into, rather than over, heavy swells. She is fitted for FuMO 21 with reconfigured bridge and removal of the forward searchlight; the radar array has been deleted by the censor.

sea. Clutching problems led to the abandonment of cruising turbines after the Type 1934. The use of synthetic plastic for propeller shaft bearings on the Type 1936A onward resulted in severe wear problems and the steel piping fitted in place of non-ferrous metals was subject to corrosion.

All these issues affected range and availability. Rather than the hoped-for ranges of 5000nm at 20kts and 7000nm at 17kts, the Type 1934 achieved 1900nm at 19kts. Availability during the war averaged 40 per cent; *Z15* spent 64 per cent of the war in dock, including eleven months from June 1940 to May 1941, with engine problems.

Armament. The decision to fit the 5.9in gun in an effort to boost firepower further compromised stability and seaworthiness by adding more weight. The single 5.9in mount weighed 6.5 tons more than the 5in single mount and while there were only four mounts fitted, the total weight gain was 15 tons, all of it up high.

The addition of the twin turret worsened the weight problem. At 66.6 tons, it was nearly twice as heavy as two single 5.9in mounts and with all the weight concentrated forward of the bridge it increased the tendency for the bows to drive into waves instead of over them. The hoped-for increase in the rate of fire was not realised as the hoists could only deliver 7–8 rounds per minute which set the maximum rate of fire to about half that attained by the 5in guns.

Both the single mounts and the turret relied solely on manual loading and the shells and charges, being 1.5 times heavier than their 5in counterparts, proved difficult to manhandle. The turret magazine hoist connected to a handing room below the turret, the ammunition had to be transferred to another hoist for delivery to the guns. These factors reduced the effective rate of fire.

The turret was not watertight and was continually exposed to heavy seas crashing aboard. Not surprisingly, it was frequently out of action due to short circuits, damaged equipment, and a soaked crew. It was also considerably delayed in development. Nine of the ships selected to be fitted with it were completed with a single 5.9in mount forward (*Z23–Z31*); the first turret was installed on *Z23* from February to June 1942. In operations in the Arctic that September the extra weight resulted in the bows diving heavily into the sea and throwing water over the bridge, leaving the turret awash. Flag Officer (Destroyers) Vice Admiral Bey was very critical and recom-

The after side of the forward funnel on an unidentified Type 1934 destroyer showing a host of details. Items of interest include both derricks, the boat chock for the motorboat, boiler room intake vents, and the funnel piping. *(US National Archives 80-G-15671 via Roger Torgeson)*

Z39 carrying a full load of mines, probably in March 1944. Note the small propeller guard, the spray strake/ degaussing cable, the quad 20mm atop the after deckhouse, the life rafts adorning No 3 mount and the extra rafts outboard of the AA deck. It is interesting to note that the German ships could carry a full load of mines without landing any equipment, unlike the British destroyers which had to land gun mounts and/or torpedo tubes

mended that the turret not be fitted to any other ships.

The net result of the armament upgrade was that ships fitted with the 5.9in gun were actually less effective combat units than the ships fitted with the 5in gun. This was recognised by the Kriegsmarine and the 1936B (Mob) class reverted to the 5in main armament.

Personnel. The Kriegsmarine was plagued with personnel problems which directly affected the destroyer's engineering departments as they struggled on their own with teething problems and the development of standard operating procedures. The Treaty of Versailles limited peacetime strength to 15,000 men, which prior to rearmament was not enough to man the shore establishments and the fleet. Once the restriction was lifted, new recruits were of poor quality due to the manpower shortages caused by rearmament in all the armed services.

Crew members posing aboard a Type 1936A or Type 1936A (Mob) giving a good view of the twin turret details: open sighting ports, ladder rungs between the barrels, life rafts, the high elevating angle, and the complex shape of the gun mount. The steel shutters have been closed on all the bridge windows.

Between the completion of *Z1* in January 1937 and *Z22* in September 1939, one new destroyer was completed approximately every six weeks. Training times had to be reduced from 26 months ashore and 28 months afloat to 13 months ashore and 18 months afloat in order to provide enough crew. Existing complements were broken up and re-assigned to provide a core of trained personnel for new construction. The frequent personnel changes made it difficult to keep a highly trained team together to operate the weapons and machinery – much time was wasted in continual drills and operational training.

For the engineering departments in particular, personnel changeover was a critical issue. Tending the high-pressure steam system required experience to deal with problems and an understanding of the interactions between steam pressure, feed water supply, super-heater temperatures, and airflow. The required level of expertise was difficult to attain; constant training and inexperienced recruits led to many mistakes when operating the temperamental high-pressure systems. Standard operating procedures only developed through informal exchanges of information between crews as part of the troubleshooting process.

On average, changeovers of personnel took place every six months and affected 30 per cent of the crew. Between September 1939 and October 1940, *Z10* had a turnover rate of 100 per cent in the engine room officers and 62 per cent of other ratings. Personnel changes continued unabated throughout the war. In October 1940, the torpedo and gunnery officers and other crew members were transferred from *Z14* and *Z16* for service aboard U-boats. This left both ships practically non-operational until replacements could be trained.

Often going unnoticed, the personnel issues were a major contributing factor to the destroyer's overall poor wartime performance.

BUILDING DATA AND FATES

Type 1934

Name	Launched	Commissioned	Builder	Fate
Z1 Leberecht Maass	18.8.1935	14.1.1937	Deutsche Werke, Kiel	Sunk in error by Luftwaffe aircraft 22.2.1940
Z2 Georg Thiele	18.8.1935	27.2.1937	Deutsche Werke, Kiel	Run aground in Rombakenfjord, Narvik 13.4.1940
Z3 Max Schultz	30.11.1935	8.4.1937	Deutsche Werke, Kiel	Mined 22.2.1940
Z4 Richard Beitzen	30.11.1935	13.5.1937	Deutsche Werke, Kiel	Broken up at Rosyth from 10.1.1949

Type 1934A

Name	Launched	Commissioned	Builder	Fate
Z5 Paul Jacobi	24.3.1936	29.6.1937	Deschimag, Bremen	To France as *Desaix* 1946
Z6 Theodor Riedel	22.4.1936	2.7.1937	Deschimag, Bremen	To France as *Kleber* 1946
Z7 Hermann Schoemann	16.7.1936	9.9.1937	Deschimag, Bremen	Sunk in action with HMS *Edinburgh* 2.5.1942
Z8 Bruno Heinemann	15.9.1936	8.1.1938	Deschimag, Bremen	Sunk after hitting two mines off Calais 25.1.1942
Z9 Wolfgang Zenker	27.3.1936	2.7.1938	Germania-Werft, Kiel	Scuttled in Rombakenfjord, Narvik 13.4.1940
Z10 Hans Lody	14.5.1936	13.9.1938	Germania-Werft, Kiel	To Britain as *R38*. Used for evaluation trials and then scrapped from 17.7.1949
Z11 Bernd Von Arnim	8.7.1936	6.12.1938	Germania-Werft, Kiel	Scuttled in Rombakenfjord, Narvik 13.4.1940
Z12 Erich Giese	12.3.1937	4.3.1939	Germania-Werft, Kiel	Sunk in action at Narvik 13.4.1940
Z13 Erich Koellner	18.3.1937	28.8.1939	Germania-Werft, Kiel	Sunk in action at Narvik 13.4.1940 while acting as a floating battery
Z14 Friedrich Ihn	5.11.1936	6.4.1938	Blohm & Voss, Hamburg	To Soviet Union as *Prytkiy* 1946
Z15 Erich Steinbrinck	24.9.1936	31.5.1938	Blohm & Voss, Hamburg	To Soviet Union as *Pylkii* 1946
Z16 Friedrich Eckholdt	21.3.1937	28.7.1938	Blohm & Voss, Hamburg	Sunk during Battle of Barents Sea 31.12.1942

Type 1936

Name	Launched	Commissioned	Builder	Fate
Z17 Diether Von Roeder	19.8.1937	29.8.1938	Deschimag, Bremen	Scuttled alongside Postpier in Narvik 13.4.1940
Z18 Hans Ludemann	1.12.1937	8.10.1938	Deschimag, Bremen	Run aground in Rombakenfjord, Narvik 13.4.1940
Z19 Hermann Kunne	22.12.1937	12.1.1939	Deschimag, Bremen	Run aground in Herjangsfjord, Narvik 13.4.1940
Z20 Karl Galster	15.6.1938	21.3.1939	Deschimag, Bremen	To Soviet Union as *Prochnyy* 1946
Z21 Wilhelm Heidkamp	20.8.1938	20.6.1939	Deschimag, Bremen	Torpedoed and sunk in Narvik harbour 10.4.1940
Z22 Anton Schmitt	20.9.1938	24.9.1939	Deschimag, Bremen	Torpedoed and sunk in Narvik harbour 10.4.1940

Type 1936A

Name	Launched	Commissioned	Builder	Fate
Z23	15.12.1939	14.9.1940	Deschimag, Bremen	CTL in air raid on La Pallice 12.8.1944. Scrapped in France from 1951
Z24	7.3.1940	23.10.1940	Deschimag, Bremen	Capsized at Bordeaux after air attack 25.8.1944
Z25	16.3.1940	30.11.1940	Deschimag, Bremen	To France as *Hoche* 1946
Z26	2.4.1940	11.1.1941	Deschimag, Bremen	Sunk in action with *Trinidad*, *Fury*, and *Eclipse* 29.3.1942
Z27	1.8.1940	26.2.1941	Deschimag, Bremen	Sunk in action with *Glasgow* and *Enterprise* 28.12.1943
Z28	20.8.1940	9.8.1941	Deschimag, Bremen	Bombed and sunk by RAF aircraft at Sassnitz 7.3.1945
Z29	15.10.1940	9.7.1941	Deschimag, Bremen	Scuttled in the Western Baltic 7.7.1946
Z30	8.12.1940	15.11.1941	Deschimag, Bremen	To Britain. Expended in explosive trials 1948

Type 1936A (Mob)

Name	Launched	Commissioned	Builder	Fate
Z31	15.5.1941	11.4.1942	Deschimag, Bremen	To France as *Marceau* 1946
Z32	15.8.1941	15.9.1942	Deschimag, Bremen	Ran aground on Ile de Bas after action with Allied destroyers 9.6.1944
Z33	15.9.1941	06.2.1943	Deschimag, Bremen	To Soviet Union as *Provornyi* 1946
Z34	05.5.1942	05.6.1943	Deschimag, Bremen	Scuttled in the Skaggerak 22.3.1946
Z37	24.2.1941	16.7.1942	Germania-Werft, Kiel	CTL after colliding with *Z32* 29.1.1944. Scrapped in France from 1949
Z38	05.8.1941	20.3.1943	Germania-Werft, Kiel	To Britain as *Nonsuch*. Expended in explosive trials 1949
Z39	02.12.1941	21.8.1943	Germania-Werft, Kiel	To USA for evaluation trials in 1945. To France for spares and then scrapped from 1953

Type 1936B (Mob)

Name	Launched	Commissioned	Builder	Fate
Z35	02.10.1942	22.9.1943	Deschimag, Bremen	Lost on German minefield off Estonia 12.12.1944
Z36	15.5.1943	19.2.1944	Deschimag, Bremen	Lost on German minefield off Estonia 12.12.1944
Z43	15.9.1943	24.3.1944	Deschimag, Bremen	Scuttled off Flensburg just north of Kiel 3.5.1945
Z44	20.1.1944		Deschimag, Bremen	Sunk while fitting out at Bremen 29.7.1944
Z45	15.4.1944		Deschimag, Bremen	Scuttled incomplete 20.7.1946

Below: *Z39* off Boston on 12 September 1945. This view shows the large winch on the quarterdeck, the AA armament on the after superstructure, and the life rafts stowed on extensions outboard of the AA deck. *(US National Archives 19-N-90596)*

Z39 IN CLOSE-UP

Z39 was the most modern of the destroyers still afloat at the end of the war and was allocated to the Americans who were interested in her high-pressure steam power plant. She was turned over to the USN at Plymouth on 12 July 1945. In company with the surrendered torpedo boat *T35* and with a mixed US-German crew aboard, she sailed via the Azores and Argentia to Boston where she arrived on 7 August.

During extensive underway machinery and manoeuvrability trials, she was commissioned into the US Navy as *DD-939* on 14 September; after enough operational experience had been gained by US crews, the German crew was sent home on the 28th. She continued with trials until November 1947 when she was declared surplus and sold to the French Navy as a source of spare parts for their ex-German destroyers. She ended her days as a pontoon for minesweepers near Brest and was broken up in 1964.

During her period in the US, she was extensively photographed – some of the detailed photos reproduced here show features common to the rest of the German destroyer fleet. *(All photos in this section by courtesy of Roger Torgeson)*

Right: Masthead details on 13 August 1945. FuMB Sumatra is fitted to the front and sides of the searchlight platform. Jutting out just above the crowsnest is a FuMB 26 Tunis antenna. Not visible at the top of the mast are FuMB Bali and FuMO 81 Berlin-S antennas. *(US National Archives NH 75385)*

Opposite: Z39 in drydock showing a host of details around the after gun deck: canvas covered quad 20mm fitted to the top of the deckhouse, the canvas screen on the back of the gun mount, the cable reels, and the frame clipped to No.3 gun enclosing the life raft, paddles, and life ring. *(US National Archives NH 75407)*

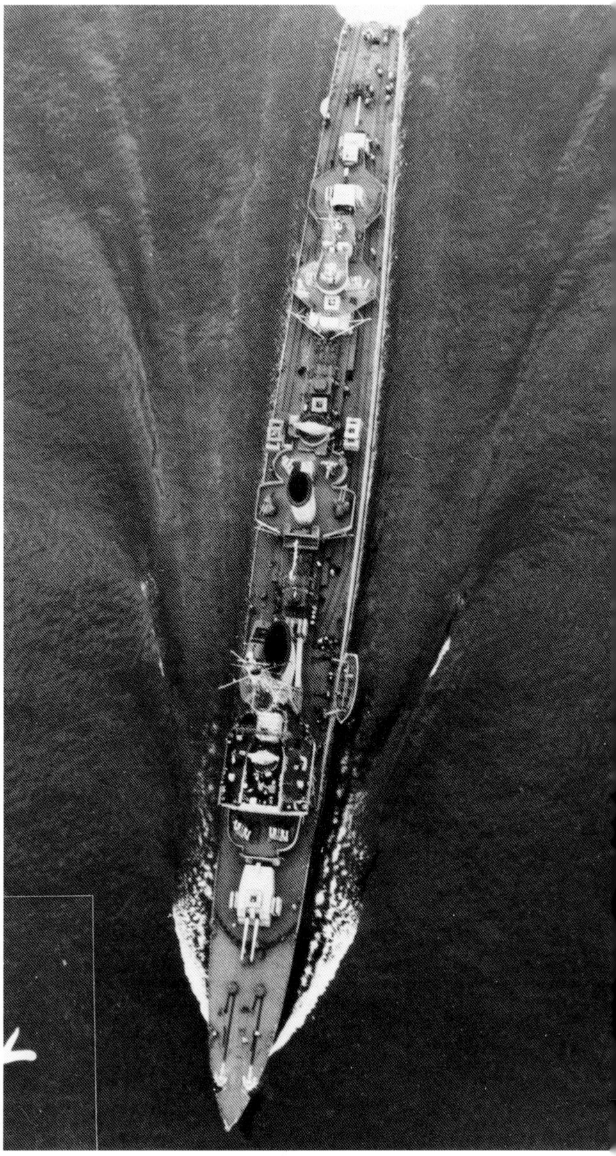

Above, left: An 11 August view showing the ground tackle details on the forecastle, twin 37mm guns, bridge front, canvas covered forward rangefinder, the massive FuMO 24/25, and the forward searchlight platform. A FuMO 81 Berlin-S radar unit is at the top of the mast. *(US National Archives NH 75382)*

Above, right: This 12 September shot provides a rarely photographed overhead view of the shape of all the decks and their fittings. Note the lighter coloured area forward of the breakwater. *(US National Archives 19-N-90599)*

Left: Detail around the after torpedo tube mounting. The control position has been fitted with a metal weather-proof cover. Note the rafts atop the front of the tubes and at the after end of the AA deck just forward, the darker colour at the forward end of the tubes, and the tie-downs preventing the mounting from training. The square canister on the main deck just aft of the open hatch is a reload torpedo locker. This area of the ship has been painted dark grey. *(US National Archives NH 75402)*

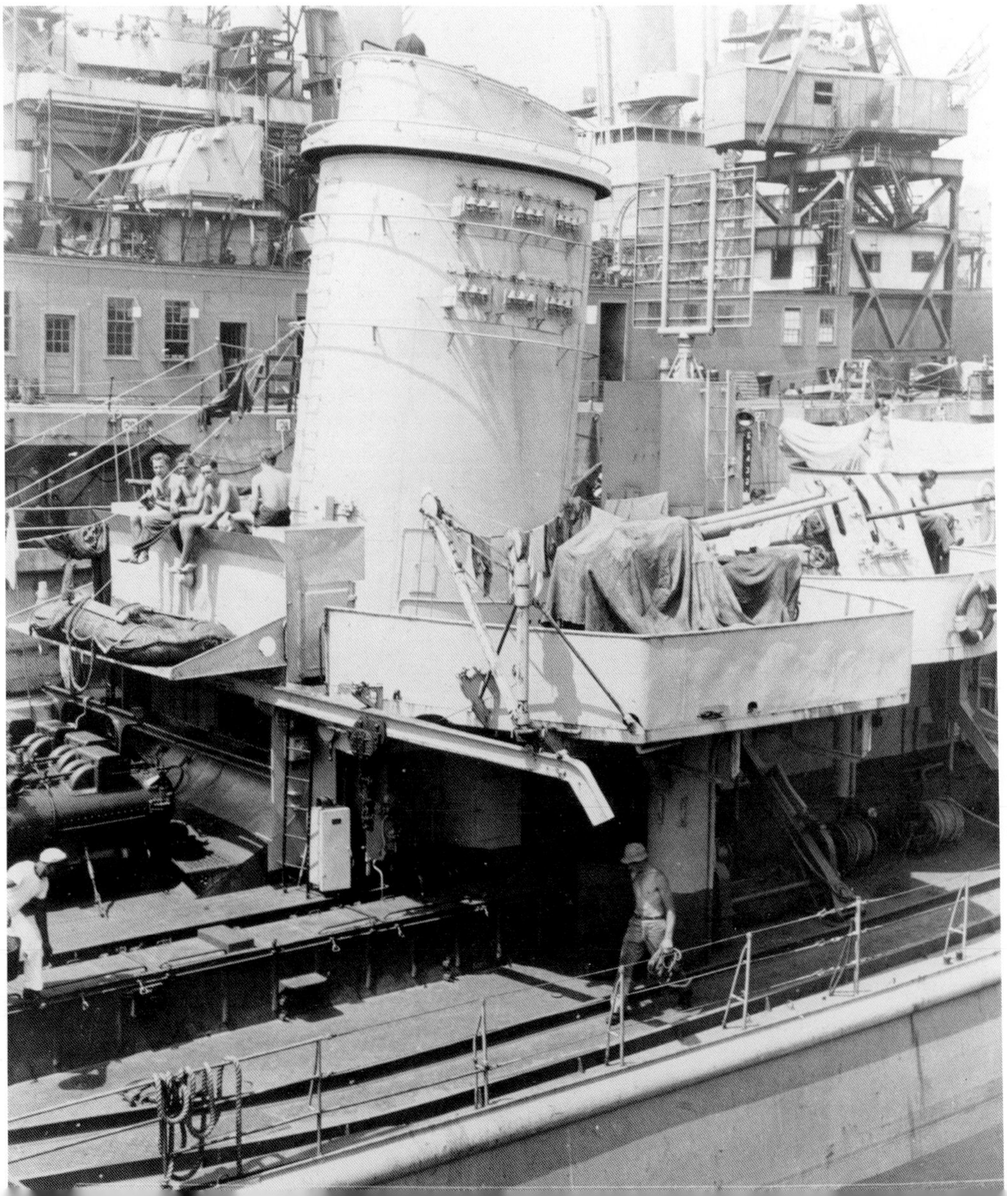

Right: This 11 August photo depicts the after funnel and AA deck. The girder at the front of the AA deck is fitted with a block and tackle boom that would be used to hoist the spare torpedo from the reload torpedo locker just below. The forward gun under canvas is a twin 37mm, the after gun is a single 37mm. Note the FuMO 63 antenna behind the funnel and the rubber raft just below the feet of the workers perched in front of the funnel. The deck colour is carried well up the side of the superstructure. *(US National Archives NH 75405)*

Model Products

The German destroyers have never been as popular with manufacturers as the much better known German battleships and heavy cruisers, but they are well represented by card, resin, and injection moulded plastic kits in scales from 1:1250 to 1:250. The first plastic kits were released in the 1960s by Eaglewall. In the 1970s, Airfix, Heller, Matchbox, and Skywave all produced injection moulded plastic kits that were state of the art for their time. Samek and HP also produced a range of resin kits.

The commercial visibility of the destroyers and the state of the art were advanced considerably by the release, starting in 2010, of an extensive range from Trumpeter and Dragon in the popular 1:700 and 1:350 scales. Both companies produce well researched high-quality kits with plenty of parts; the Dragon kits are more complex.

Thanks to the popularity of the Trumpeter and Dragon kits, there are many aftermarket accessories available, giving modellers considerable choice appropriate to their skill level and desired level of detail.

REVIEW SUMMARY:

Manufacturer	Kit	Scale	Year	Parts	Etch Parts	Detail	Accuracy	Complexity
Hansa	Type 1934	1250	1970	1	None	4	3	5
Hansa	Type 1936A (Mob)	1250	1970	1	None	4	3	5
Eaglewall	*Diether von Roeder*	1200	1960	37	None	5	4	5
Eaglewall	*Leberecht Maass*	1200	1960	34	None	5	4	5
Dragon	*Z31*	700	2011	286	54	1	1	1
Dragon	*Z39*	700	2011	177	54	1	1	1
Revell	*Z38*	700	2011	72	None	3	3	4
Samek	*Z28*	700		91	23	2	1	3
Skywave	Secret Base	700		329	None	3	3	4
Tamiya	Z Class	700	1997	65	None	3	3	4
Trumpeter	*Z7* 1942	700	2013	223	10	1	2	3
Trumpeter	*Z21* 1940	700	2012	237	13	1	1	3
Trumpeter	*Z25* 1944	700	2011	242	18	1	1	3
Trumpeter	*Z28* 1945	700	2012	244	16	1	1	3
Trumpeter	*Z30* 1942	700	2012	242	17	1	1	3
Trumpeter	*Z43* 1944	700	2012	248	15	1	1	3
Airfix	Narvik (*Z28*)	600	1974	94	None	3	2	3
Heller	*Z31* 1942	400		209	None	2	2	3
Dragon	*Z31*	350	2011	666	183	1	1	1
Dragon	*Z39*	350	2011	511	191	1	1	1
Revell	Type 1936	350	2016	179	None	1	1	3
Trumpeter	*Z25* 1944	350	2010	386	58	1	1	3
Trumpeter	*Z30* 1942	350	2011	380	93	1	1	3
Trumpeter	*Z43* 1944	350	2011	376	93	1	1	3
JSC	*Z32*	250			None	1	1	3
Wilhelmshavener	Type 1936A	250			None	1	1	3

Note: For Detail, Accuracy, and Complexity, 1 marks the highest end of the scale and 5 the lowest

HANSA

1:1250 Scale

Hansa produced a large line of die-cast model ships in the 1970s–1980s which were usually sold ready-built and painted, including Type 1934A and 1936A (Mob) destroyers. Quite detailed for their physical size, they remain highly collectible today.

Photo courtesy of **Jeffrey Stevenson**

Z38

EAGLEWALL

1:1200 Scale

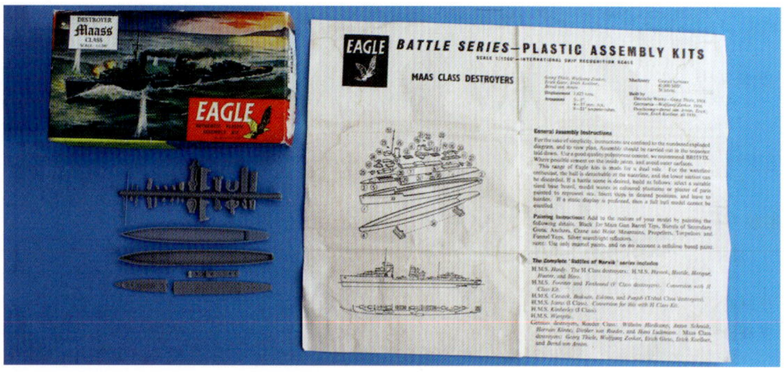

Eagle *Leberecht Maass* kit contents

Kits of *Leberecht Maass* and *Diether von Roeder* were produced by Eaglewall Plastics in 1960 as part of a larger series of constant 1:1200 scale warships, which could be built full hull or waterline. Despite their small size, these two kits are quite distinct with differing funnels, superstructure, and decks. Complete, boxed, unbuilt kits are highly prized by ship kit collectors.

Photo courtesy of **Jeffrey Stevenson**

TAMIYA

1:700 Scale

The kit contains two identical destroyers and depicts a Type 1936A (Mob) as built and is the same kit once produced by Skywave in the 1970s, except the Skywave aircraft are NOT included in this re-release.

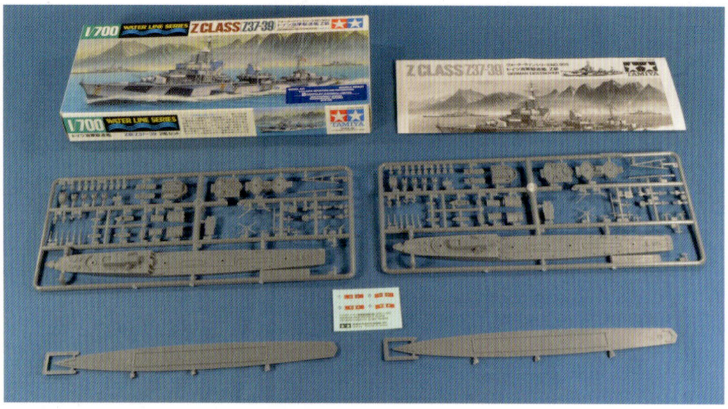

Tamiya Z class kit contents

There are some challenges with the kit: there is no detail on the hull or superstructure sides, the main guns and AA guns are rudimentary, there are no davits for the boats, no reload torpedo lockers, the AA deck is the incorrect shape and the bow is raked too sharply. The instructions switch the positions of the forward rangefinder (which should be on the bridge) and the forward quad 20mm (which should be in front of the bridge). Adequate in its day, the kit has been overtaken by better offerings.

Review kit courtesy of **Neil Ramage**

REVELL

1:700 Scale

The kit depicts *Z38* in 1943 with spray strake forward but prior to being fitted with a quad 20mm ahead of the bridge, and is the same kit once produced by Matchbox in the 1970s.

The kit does have some problems: the AA deck is incorrectly shaped, the forward gun platform is for the single 5.9in, the boats are attached to the underside of the AA deck, the forward funnel cowl and forecastle break are not curved, and there is no quad 20mm aft, degaussing cable, reload torpedo lockers, raised mine rails, or life rafts. It will be a challenge to correct the issues, but it is an easy build. Three camouflage schemes are provided in the instructions for *Z31*, *Z33*, and *Z37*.

Revell *Z38* kit contents

DRAGON

1:700 Scale

Dragon offer two related kits, one depicting *Z31* as she appeared from

Dragon *Z39* kit contents

1942 to August 1944, with the single 5.9in on a raised platform forward and weather shields fitted to the torpedo mounts. Dragon provides two hulls – one waterline and one full hull. The full hull features bilge keels and an S-Gerät dome; both hulls have portholes and propeller guards.

To give an idea of the detail, there are eleven pieces for the foremast and the mast is tapered; sixteen pieces make up the upper bridge. Dragon uses a common weapons sprue with one 5.9in mount; four are provided leaving plenty of leftover smaller fittings for the parts box. There is also an etch set, a decal sheet and the instruction sheet shows two different colour schemes. The only minor problem is the lack of a degaussing cable and for absolute accuracy the radar should be FuMO 21.

The second kit – of *Z39* in April 1945 after her Barbara upgrade – contains the identical parts found in the *Z31* kit except that the main deck is configured for the twin turret forward, the forward superstructure is shorter and the after deckhouse is larger. Both hulls included feature the combined spray strake/degaussing cable that *Z39* carried at the main deck level around the entire hull. The etch set is the same in both kits.

SAMEK

1:700 Scale

Below: Samek *Z28* kit contents

This resin kit depicts *Z28* in her 1942 fit with relocated mainmast, a single quad 20mm on the after deckhouse, no spray strake, and weather shields on the torpedo tubes. The one-piece hull is complete with the lower parts of the forward, amidships, and after superstructure and has plenty of detail. The bridge decks, AA deck, funnels, torpedo tubes, boats, life rafts, and top of the after deckhouse are separate castings. The main guns have separate barrels, and there are weather shields for the torpedo tubes. There is an etch set consisting of boat davits, derrick booms, propeller guards, stern cranes, anchors, FuMO 21, and the single and quad 20mm guns. Patterns are supplied for the masts.

Detail throughout is good but careful study is required to track down the positions of all the smaller parts. The colour scheme on the box matches one applied to *Z29*; it is not known if it was worn by *Z28*.

Below: Close-up of bridge decks, AA deck, funnels, and after deckhouse

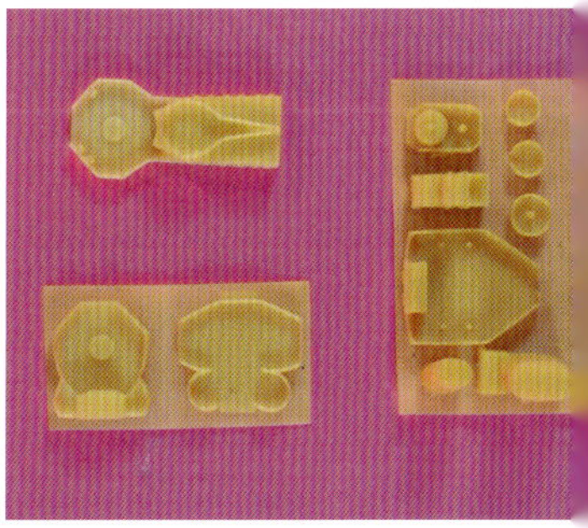

TRUMPETER

1:700 Scale

While the six 1:700 scale Trumpeter kits reviewed here are from four different classes, they all share a number of common and similar features. Common to all are two identical sprues containing the 5in and 5.9in gun mounts, torpedo tubes, boats, derricks, rafts, and a host of smaller fittings. Each kit also has a full colour painting diagram with references for the Mr Hobby, Vallejo, Model Master, Tamiya, and Humbrol ranges. There are two photo-etch frets, one with a display stand and name plate; the other contains kit specific parts. The instructions are in booklet form and show each of the enclosed sprues and frets. There is a set of flag decals. In addition, *Z25*, *Z28*, *Z30*, and *Z43* all share two other sprues which contain the main deck with moulded-in torpedo reload lockers, lower bridge deck, superstructure sides and decks, funnels, underwater fittings, masts, 5.9in twin turret, and numerous other fittings. *Z25*, *Z28*, and *Z30* all have the same hull. Each kit has its own unique sprue of parts which includes a name plate.

Features similar to all are a one piece upper hull with portholes and propeller guards; there is also a lower hull and waterline plate. The decks all feature moulded-in mine rails, anchor chains, and breakwaters; the bridge decks have moulded-in planking and the funnels are one piece. The superstructure sides have hatches, vents, and ports; there are seven mines for the mine rails. The quality of mouldings is excellent throughout, with many fine details, very delicate small fittings, and precise fit. There will be plenty of spares for the parts box. Individual kits are as follows:

Z7 1942. This kit actually depicts *Z7* as she appeared from completion in September 1937 until mid-1938, as it has the rounded bridge front first fitted. In addition to the mis-labelled time period, there are some inaccuracies: the hull is fitted with a spray strake which *Z7* did not carry and the propeller guards should be larger and higher on the hull. There are no pipes at the rear of the forward funnel and the forecastle break plating does not have the square cut at the bottom. The colour diagram shows a camouflage scheme which the ship would not have carried in peacetime. This kit can be used for *Z5* and *Z6* which both had the rounded bridge front when first completed.

Box art for Trumpeter *Z7* 1942

Z21 1940 as completed with Atlantic bows, rangefinder in a tub at the back of the bridge, and no degaussing cable. The box art shows the ship with a peacetime tactical number of 21 and a degaussing cable, but

Above: Box art for Trumpeter *Z21* 1940

Right: Trumpeter *Z30* 1942 kit contents

Z21's tactical number was 43, and she never wore it while fitted with a degaussing cable. Only the port side mine rails are fitted and they only go part way to the stern from the forecastle break. The etch set has the foremast aerial spreader, foremast searchlight platform, bulwarks, funnel grills, and capstan tops. This kit can be used for *Z20* after the February 1940 refit which moved the TAM forward on the bridge.

***Z25* 1944** fitted with the 5.9in turret after the completion of her 'Barbara' AA upgrade in late 1944 with subsequent alterations to the AA fit. She is also fitted with a spray strake, weather shielded torpedo tube control positions, FuMO 21 forward, FuMO 63 behind the after funnel, two cutters, and one motorboat with derrick. To be strictly accurate for this time frame, the single guns on the AA deck should be 20mm, and the forward radar should be FuMO 24/25. This kit can be used for any of the Type 1936A fitted with the twin turret.

Below: Box art for Trumpeter *Z28* 1945

Right: Trumpeter *Z43* 1944 kit contents

***Z28* 1945** with two quad 20mm on the after deckhouse, two 37mm singles abaft No 2 mount, spray strake, weather shielded torpedo tube control positions, FuMO 24/25 forward and FuMO 63 behind the after funnel. The etch set has shields for the 37mm singles, funnel grills, shields for the quad 20mm, both types of radar aerials, foremast aerial spreader, foremast searchlight platform, and capstan tops.

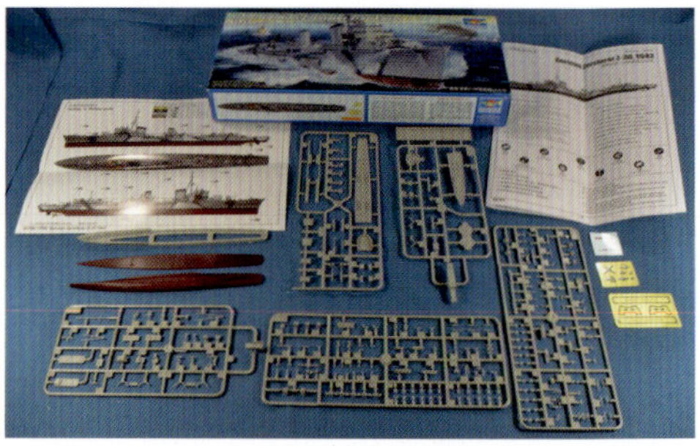

***Z30* 1942** as she appeared shortly after entering service with four 5.9in single mounts and catwalks over the torpedo tubes. She is also fitted with a spray strake, weather shielded torpedo tube control positions, FuMO 21 forward, the after searchlight, two cutters, and one motorboat with derrick.

It is not clear if *Z30* was ever fitted with a spray strake, and certainly wasn't in 1942. The shielded torpedo control positions may not have been fitted at this time either; the alternate open positions are included in the kit. This kit can be used for any of the Type 1936A fitted with the forward single 5.9in mount.

***Z43* 1944** as she appeared when completed with five 5in single mounts and the designed AA and boat fits. The combined spray strake/degaussing cable at the main deck level is present and a FuMO 21 radar aerial is fitted on the bridge. This class was not fitted with FuMO 21, so for accuracy the radar aerial could be replaced with the larger FuMO 24/25. This kit can be used for any of the Type 1936B (Mob).

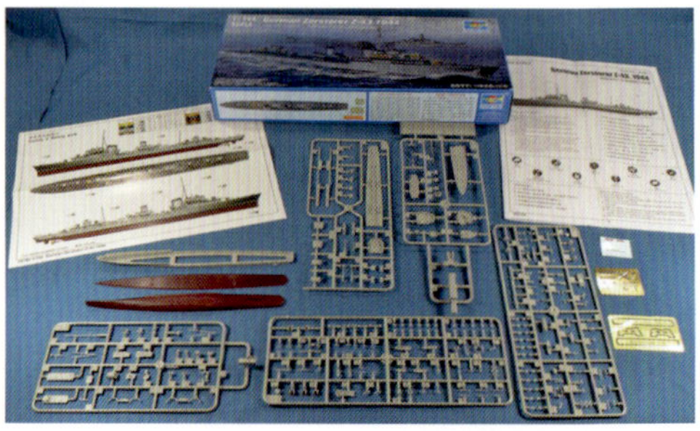

Skywave German Base kit contents

SKYWAVE 1:700 Scale

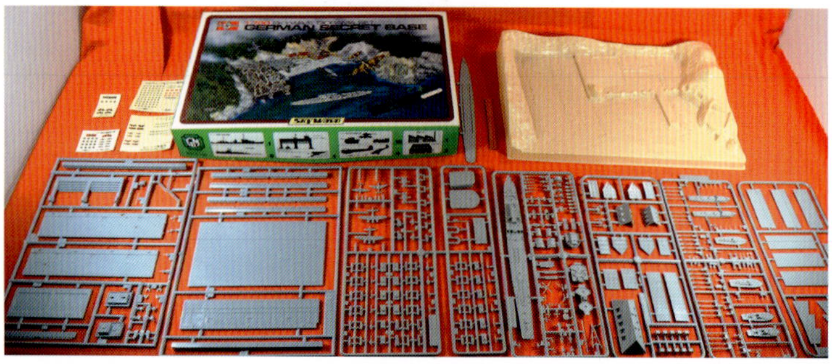

The 'German Secret Base' kit has everything needed to create a small naval base suitable for displaying any German navy destroyer. It contains one sprue of each of the following Skywave kits: Z class destroyer (*see Tamiya Z Class review*), U-Boat bunker, European Buildings, Factory Buildings, Torpedo Boats (*S-Boat, PT Boat,* and *Vosper*), and Panzer Division tanks and vehicles. The diorama base is made from styrene and contains cut-outs for the U-Boat bunker and buildings, and a wharf and oil storage tank. Assembly instructions are provided for each of the kits. Although it has long been out of production, this kit is one that is well worth searching for.

■ Review kit courtesy of **Neil Ramage**

AIRFIX

1:600 Scale

Airfix Narvik class kit contents

Although sold as a 'Narvik' class destroyer, this kit specifically depicts *Z28* in her 1944 fit with the mainmast relocated to the front of the after deckhouse, a spray strake, and a quad 20mm atop the after deckhouse. The hull, superstructure, and funnels are all split port and starboard; the hull halves have a line inscribed on the inside to be used as a guide if the modeller wishes to cut away the lower hull.

The kit is well detailed with a clearly defined degaussing cable, capstans, funnel grills, boiler room intakes, FuMO 21 radar, torpedo tubes, depth charge throwers, and mine rails; the torpedo tubes have the weather shields over the control positions. The propeller guards are too large. There is no port side motor boat, with two moulded-in life rafts in its place; the starboard side motor boat and derrick, and the two amidships cutters are present.

First released in 1974, this kit was, and still is, very impressive, but the injection pin marks on the superstructure and funnels, and the rather rudimentary AA guns reflect the state of the art at the time the kit was produced. It is a pity that Airfix chose to model the only unique German destroyer, so using this kit to depict any of the other ships will require extensive conversion.

HELLER

1:400 Scale

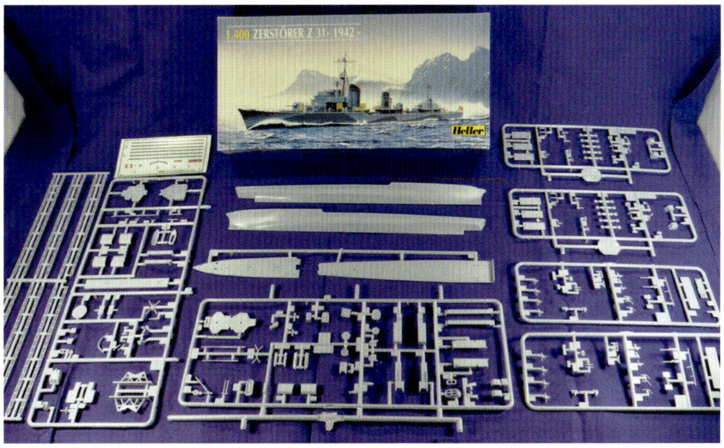

Heller *Z31* 1942 kit contents

Despite the 1942 date on the box, this kit depicts *Z31* as she appeared for a brief period during 1944 with the quad 20mm and single 5.9in mount forward, FuMO 24/25 radar, and weather shields on the torpedo tubes. The full hull, superstructure pieces, funnels, and two of the boats, are all split into port and starboard halves. Moulded-in detail includes portholes, bilge keels, and degaussing cable on the hull, hatches, ports and ladders on the superstructure, steam pipes on the funnels, mine rails on the main deck, radar array, and deck planking on the lower bridge deck. The decal sheet includes striping for the boot topping along the waterline, flags, and the aircraft recognition marker for the forecastle.

The only items requiring some attention are the AA deck, which is the wrong shape, the reload torpedo lockers are not present, and the gun platform for the forward 5.9in mount should be connected to the forward deckhouse by a raised platform. The 5.9in mounts could be opened at the back. This kit can be used for any of the Type 1936A (Mob) if using the twin turret.

DRAGON

1:350 Scale

Dragon offer two 1:350 scale kits of the same two vessels available in 1:700 – *Z31* in the 1942 to August 1944 fit, and *Z39* in April 1945 after her Barbara upgrade. Both contain a plethora of plastic and etch parts, allowing an immense level of detail. As examples, the reload torpedo lockers are separate pieces, there are 15 cable reels of three different sizes, the hatches on the superstructure are separate pieces and can be assembled opened or closed, the lower bridge platform has separate bulwarks and six pieces of equipment – including two captain's chairs – there are ten individual mines each made up of eight parts, the 37mm guns are made from 14 parts and include seats for the gunners, the quad 20mm has 13 parts and seats for its gunners; there are even six figures for placing on the finished model. The

Dragon *Z31* kit contents (the hull is shown assembled and painted)

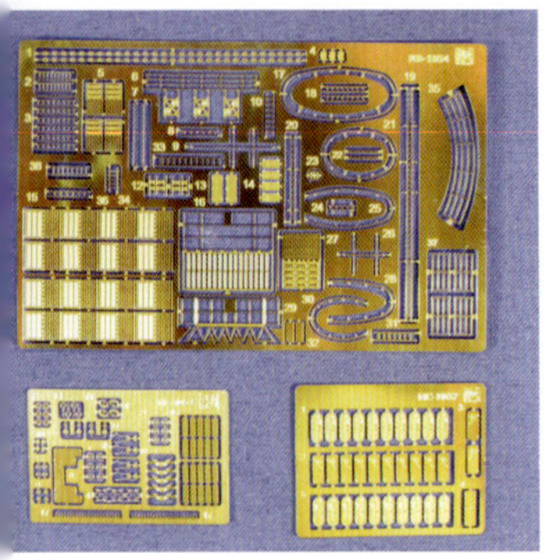

Photo-etch sheets

moulded-on detail is also considerable, down to raised rivets on the open backed gun mounts.

The hull is split into an upper and a lower hull; there is no waterline plate for those wishing to make the waterline version. The lower hull has bilge keels, an S-Gerät dome, and boiler room intakes; the propeller guards are separate pieces. For *Z31*, the only minor problem is the lack of a degaussing cable and for absolute accuracy the radar should be FuMO 21.

Dragon *Z39* kit contents

With the *Z39* kit the upper hull has the combined spray strake/degaussing cable at the main deck level, and the twin turret is on a separate weapons sprue. There are no mines included with this kit, but more of the parts on the common weapons sprues are used as *Z39* was fitted with an additional type of twin 37mm mount (14 parts), single 37mm mounts (13 parts), and twin 20mm mounts (9 parts). The AA deck twin 37mm and the quad 20mm are the same for both kits. The box art is the same as the 1:700 scale versions for both kits.

The instructions are in fold-out form, consisting of many sub-assemblies and reflect the differences between the kits; two paint schemes are provided for each with references to the Model Master, Hobby Colour, and Mr Colour ranges.

REVELL 1:350 Scale

The Type 1936 kit depicts the first three Type 1936 destroyers as built before being fitted with bilge keels; it is the same kit as the *Diether von Roeder* produced by Zvedza in 2013, now boxed and marketed by Revell. The full hull, superstructure pieces, funnels, and two of the boats, are all split into port and starboard halves. Moulded-in detail includes portholes on the hull, hatches, ports, ladders, and intake vents on the superstructure, mine rails on the main deck, and deck planking on the bridge decks. The bridge sports the pre-war eagle on its face.

Revell Type 1936 kit contents

There is a lot of detail packed into this kit with many finely produced smaller parts. The main gun mounts have detail on their fronts, have separate barrels, and they are open at the back. The torpedo tubes are well detailed with separate control positions. There are even 16 mines on trolleys and an interesting display stand portraying a rocky sea bed. Surprisingly there are no life rafts. The only minor problem is the single rudder, the Type 1936 having two. To make any of the destroyers as they appeared at Narvik it will be necessary to add bilge keels and for *Z17* a degaussing cable. This kit can be used for *Z17*, *Z18*, or *Z19*.

■ Review kit courtesy of **Revell Germany**

TRUMPETER

1:350 Scale

Trumpeter offer three of their 1:700 subjects in 1:350 scale kits featuring the same level of standardization as their 1:700 counterparts. Common to all are two identical sprues containing the 5in and 5.9in gun mounts, torpedo tubes, rafts, AA guns, and a host of smaller fittings, even single torpedoes and two individual mines are included. Multiple sprues of each are in each kit so there will be plenty of spares for the parts box. The full colour painting diagram has references for the Mr Hobby, Vallejo, Model Master, Tamiya, and Humbrol ranges. The instructions are in booklet form with 13 or 14 sub-assemblies and show each of the enclosed sprues and frets. There is a set of flag decals and a display stand. The hull is one piece with upper and lower hull; those wishing to make a waterline version will have to cut off the lower hull.

***Z25* 1944** and ***Z30* 1942** share the same hull and a sprue with the main deck, lower bridge deck, derrick, bulwarks, masts, superstructure, and radar array. *Z30* and ***Z43* 1944** have the same etch sets. The 1:350 kits are not just scaled up versions of the 1:700 kits, and what was moulded-on detail has now become individual parts for breakwater, cable reels, ammunition lockers, propeller guards, and reload torpedo lockers. The many smaller fittings are crisply moulded. Additional moulded-in detail is also extensive.

Trumpeter *Z30* 1942 kit contents

For *Z25* the single guns on the AA deck are 37mm – to be strictly accurate they should be 20mm; the radar should also be FuMO 24/25. This kit can be used for any of the Type 1936A fitted with the twin turret.

The *Z30* kit depicts the destroyer as completed with four 5.9in single mounts, catwalks over the torpedo tubes, spray strake, weather shielded torpedo tube control positions, FuMO 21 forward, the after searchlight, two cutters, and one motorboat with derrick. To be strictly accurate for this period, the spray strake should be removed, and the torpedo control positions should not have the weather shields; the alternate open positions are included in the kit. This kit can be used for any of the Type 1936A fitted with the forward single 5.9in mount.

The *Z43* kit is as she appeared when completed with five 5in single mounts, the designed AA and boat fits, combined spray strake/degaussing cable at the main deck level and a FuMO 24/25 radar array on the bridge. This kit can be used for any of the Type 1936B (Mob).

Box art for Trumpeter *Z25* 1944

WILHELMSHAVENER

1:250 Scale

This card model contains parts to build one of six ships of the 1936A (Mob) class: *Z32*, *Z33*, *Z34*, *Z37*, *Z38* or *Z39*. The components come on four sheets of A3 size card in the standard dark hull and light upper superstructure colour scheme; a fifth A3 size sheet has the parts that are unique to each ship. There are eight pages of assembly diagrams and six pages (one for each ship) showing where to place the differing parts for each. The instructions are in German with an abbreviated translation in English; the kit is packaged in a simple packet with no cover. Construction complexity is rated as Intermediate.

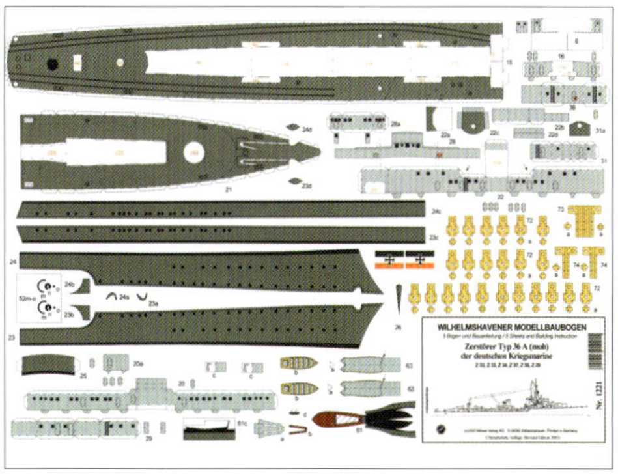

Hull, main decks, superstructure, and life rafts

■ Photo courtesy of **Les Brown**

Above: JSC Z32 Cover

Right: Forward section of hull and forecastle deck

JSC

1:250 Scale

This card model depicts *Z32* in 1943 wearing her distinctive 'vanishing point' camouflage scheme. There are six pages of components, one of which is printed on both sides so that parts like the open gun shields are coloured on the inside when assembled. The kit comes in an A4 size book with three pages of instructions in Polish with an English translation, a brief history of the ship, and assembly diagrams on the inside of the cover.

Photos courtesy of **Les Brown**

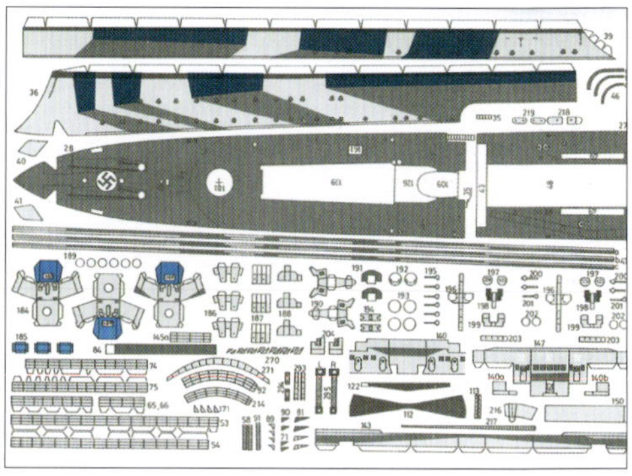

Accessories

FLYHAWK

1:700 Scale

FlyHawk supply a wide range of after-market parts for improving German destroyer kits. The following is a summary of what is available:

German Naval 2cm C/30 AA MG & 2cm Flakvierling II etch sets. The 2cm C/30 AA MG set has 60 single 20mm guns of two slightly different types, the 2cm Flakvierling has 11 non-shielded and 11 shielded quad 20mm mounts. The guns in both sets consist of multiple parts and will provide highly detailed replacement gun mounts.

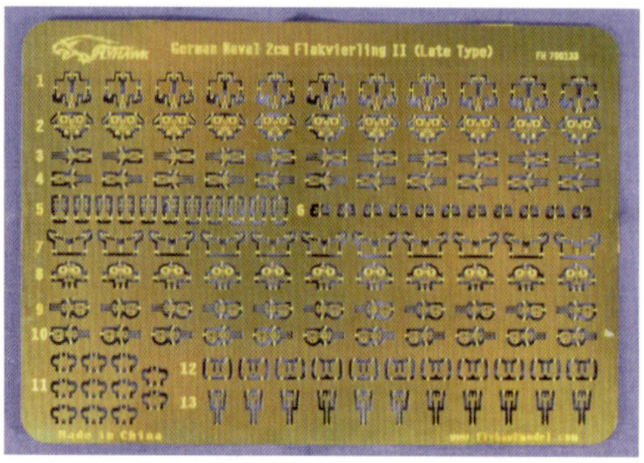

FlyHawk German Naval 2cm Flakvierling II set

15cm/48 Gun Mounts. Packaged in a sturdy plastic box, this multi-media set contains four 5.9in single gun mounts. The gun mounts are cast resin and have an open backed shield with very fine raised detail; the separate base incorporates the actual gun mounting. The gun barrels are tapered machined brass.

German Naval Weapons I & II etch sets. These sets contain the light flak armament used aboard the German destroyers. Set Weapons I has 32 single 20mm (2 parts each), 15 twin 20mm (3 parts each), and 20 single 37mm (2 parts each). There are also 12 stands (2 parts each) for the 20mm guns. Set Weapons II has 10 single 20mm (3 parts each), 18 twin 20mm with shields (3 parts each), and 22 single 37mm (3 parts each).

WW2 German Radar I & II etch sets. These high quality and comprehensive sets feature many of the radar sets used aboard German warships in World War II, including the main types found aboard the

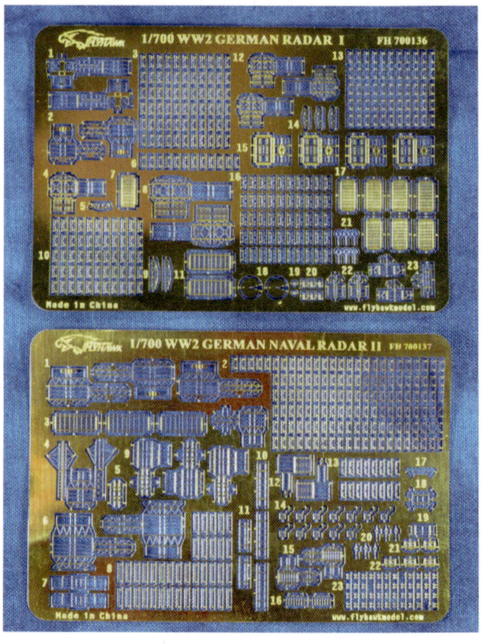

FlyHawk WW2 German Radar I and II sets

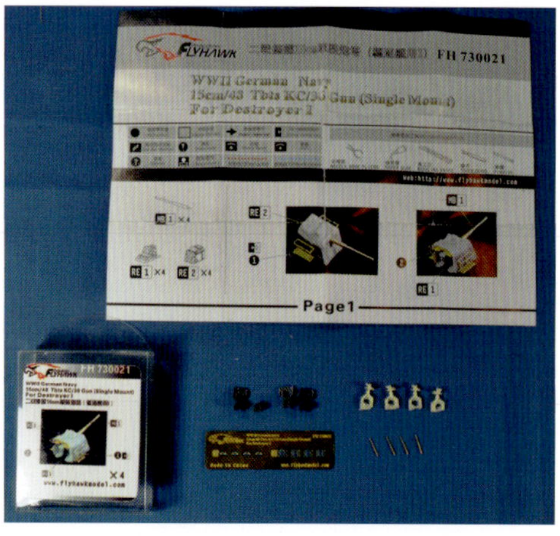

FlyHawk 15cm/48 Gun Mounts

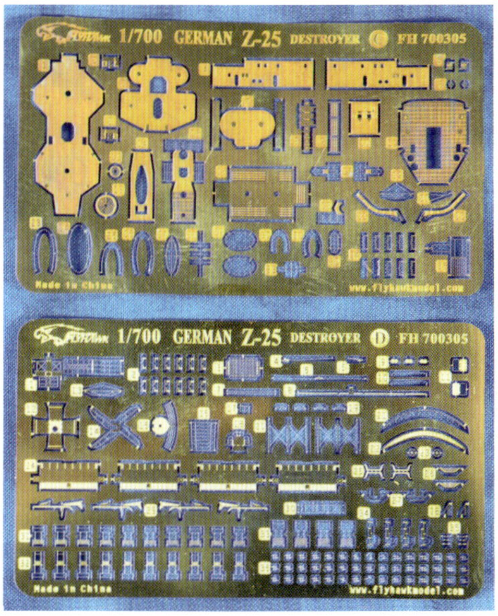

Left: FlyHawk *Z25* etch sheets C & D

Above: FlyHawk *Z25* detail set box

destroyers. Set Radar I has four FuMO 21 of two different types (two parts each), six FuMB 3 Bali (one part each), and three FuMB 6 Palau (one part each). Set Radar II has three FuMO 24/25 (two parts each), two FuMO 63 (one part each), twelve FuMB 4 Sumatra (one part each), and six FuMB Metox (one part each).

Z7* 1942 / *Z25* 1944 / *Z39 Detail sets. Those wishing to fully outfit the Trumpeter *Z7* 1942 and *Z25* 1944 and Dragon *Z39* kits will find everything they need in these extensive multi-media detail sets. Packaged in sturdy boxes, the sets consist of multiple photo-etch sheets along with resin and machined brass parts. Each set is unique with parts tailored for each kit although there are many common parts. The most striking features in each set are the brass replacement decks for all decks, which feature a textured anti-skid surface or planking for the bridge decks with cut-outs to fit over existing kit detail.

These are very high quality sets featuring plenty of relief etching; a double-sided full colour instruction sheet with precise folding instructions is included featuring detailed drawings and photographs indicating which kit parts are affected.

■ All review sets courtesy of **FlyHawk Model**

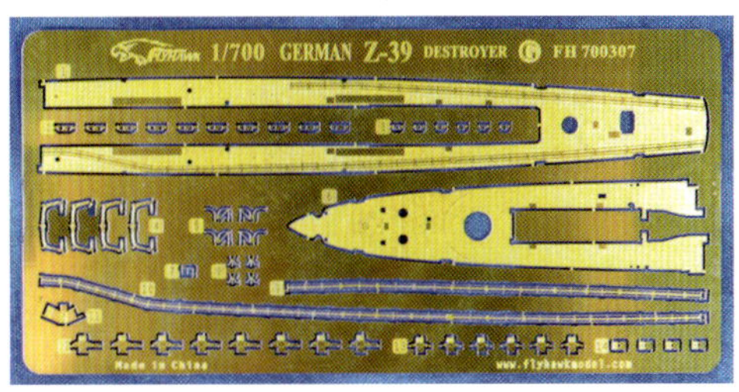

FlyHawk *Z39* etch sheet G with main decks

TOM'S MODELWORKS

1:700 Scale

The **German Destroyers** etch set is very comprehensive, providing plenty of replacement or enhancement parts, including railings, ladders, life rafts, three types of propeller guards, cable reels, a bridge eagle for the pre-war destroyers, gun shields, and radar aerials. While the parts can be used for any of the German destroyer kits, part replacement numbers are given for the Dragon *Z39*, Trumpeter *Z25 1944*, and Tamiya Z class.

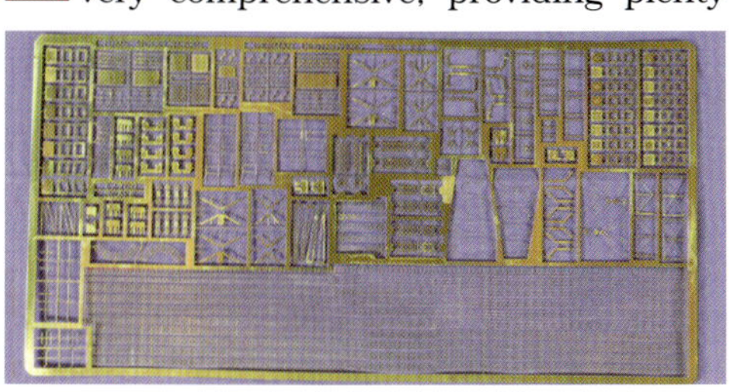

Tom's Modelworks German Destroyers Detail set

■ Review set courtesy of **Tom's Modelworks**

STARLING MODELS

1:700 Scale

German Navy Railings/Doors etch sets. There are 33 sections of 3-bar railing on the railing set, of varied pattern, and two sections of 1-bar railing. The watertight door set is comprehensive, with several different types of doors, in open or closed positions. Each features raised relief with raised hatch coamings, hinges, and handles

■ Review sets courtesy of **Starling Models**

Starling Models German Navy Railings and Doors

3DMODELPARTS

1:700 Scale

3DModelparts twin 37mm

The 3D printing process makes it possible to produce exquisitely detailed small parts without the need for moulds or casting and it is starting to revolutionize the model manufacturing business, particularly in the area of aftermarket replacement parts. This 3DModelparts **Twin 37mm SK C/30** set contains nine mounts, each of two parts: the gun mount and the twin gun barrels, which can be glued at any angle. Printed on a thin wafer, the parts come well packaged in a small tube with a card showing how the mounting looks when assembled. Use cyanoacrylate (CA) or white glue to assemble the parts. They can be painted with enamels or acrylics.

■ Review parts courtesy of **Starling Models**

WHITE ENSIGN

1:350 Scale

The impressive **Narvik Type** etch set from White Ensign is designed for the Trumpeter *Z25* 1944, *Z30* 1942, and *Z43* 1944 kits. The set features pre-cut lengths of deck railings, cable reels, funnel grills and handrails, radar aerials, mine rails, paravane detail parts, gun deck netting, etc. There are two single 40mm Bofors (10 parts each), four twin 37mm (each 6 parts), four single 20mm, four twin 20mm, two quad 20mm. Many of the parts feature relief etching. While most of the parts are generic and can be used on any of the three kits, the shape of the after gun deck on *Z43* differed from the other two; the set provides railings to fit either shape.

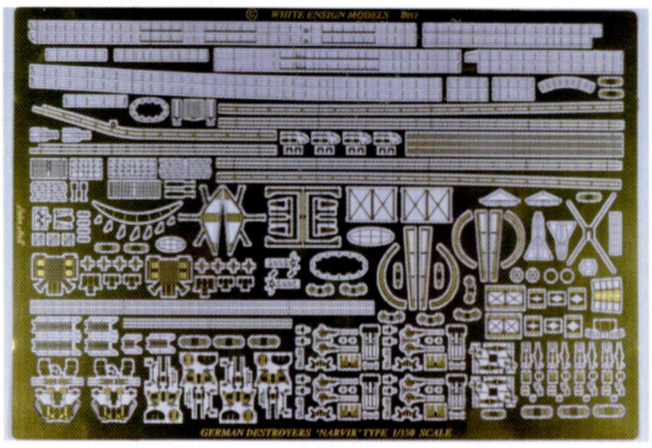

White Ensign Narvik Type Detail set

■ Review set courtesy of **Tom's Modelworks**

TOM'S MODELWORKS

1:350 Scale

The extensive **German Naval Radars** etch set includes the main types used on the destroyers in addition to the major radar sets found aboard German World War II battleships and cruisers. There are two FuMO 21 (3 parts), a single FuMO 24/25 (3 parts), two FuMO 31/63 (3 parts), four FuMB 4 Sumatra (2 parts), and a single FuMB 6 Palau (6 parts). Individual dipoles are provided for the three FuMO arrays as well as protective lattice covers for the FuMO 21 and FuMO 24/25. Two double-sided instruction sheets give precise folding and assembly instructions along with notes regarding which sets were used on which types of ships.

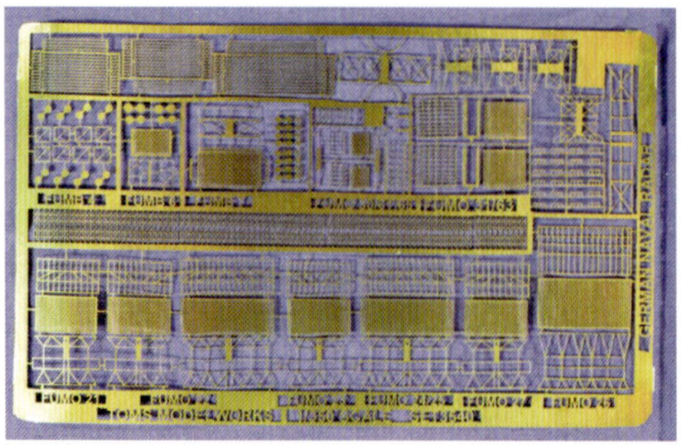

Tom's Modelworks German Naval Radar set

■ Review set courtesy of **Tom's Modelworks**

WHITE ENSIGN

1:350 Scale

Designed specifically for the Revell Type 1936 destroyer kit, WEM's **Destroyers 1936 Type** etch set contains a large assortment of parts with many featuring relief etching, including pre-cut lengths of deck railings, FuMO 21 radar, FuMO 24/25 radar, FuMO 63 radar, FuMB 4 Sumatra, funnel grills and handrails, mine rails, cable reels, capstan wheels, open torpedo control positions, goalpost foremast frame, bridge wing supports, boat cradles and thwarts, propeller guards, torpedo reload gantry booms, foremast aerial spreader, deck hatches, two twin 37mm, six single 20mm, two quad 20mm, life raft gratings, motor boat canopy and windows, vertical ladders, inclined ladders, gun deck netting, watertight doors, and anchor chain. Note that only *Z20* of this class carried radar and a quad 20mm. There are five pages of folding and assembly instructions. Modellers should encounter no problems using this well-designed set.

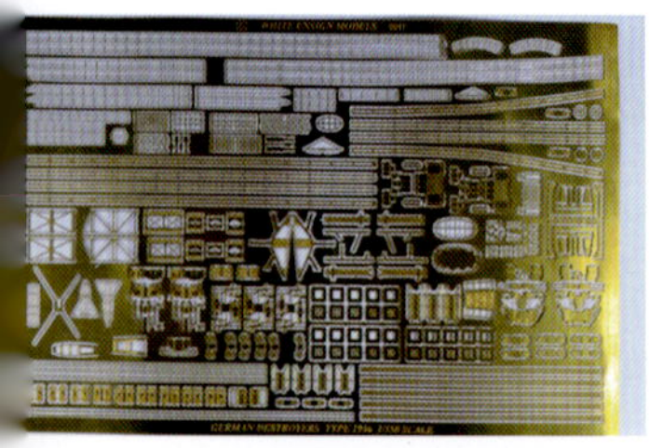

White Ensign Type 1936 Detail set

■ Review set courtesy of **Tom's Modelworks**

HUNTER

1:700 & 1:350 Scales

Deck masks considerably ease the tedium of masking off the deck prior to painting the hull and superstructure as they are manufactured to precisely fit the decks of a particular kit while leaving deck detail such as hatches and breakwaters exposed for painting. A sharp knife is all that is needed to lift the lo-tack pieces off the backing sheet. The Hunter ***Z21* 1940 deck mask** is for the 1:700 Trumpeter kit and features nine pieces on one sheet; a single page of instructions shows the kit part where each piece is to be fitted.

Hunter also produce **wood deck** sets for the Trumpeter 1:700 kits *Z30* 1942 and *Z37* 1943. Duplicates of each piece are included, allowing two kits to be upgraded from each set. Both sets also include anchor chain and a photo-etch sheet with 18 cable reels in three different sizes. The deck sheets are very thin wood and feature finely detailed deck planking. Cut-outs for hatches and deck detail are to be punched out with a sharp knife; the peel-and-stick backing is used to attach the deck pieces to the model. A simple instruction sheet with folding instructions for the cable reels and photos of the installed deck are included.

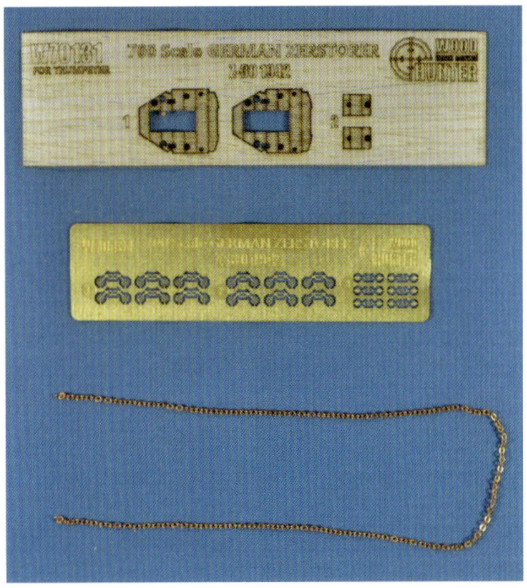

Hunter *Z30* wood deck set

There is a similar Hunter wood deck set for the Trumpeter kit *Z43 1944* in 1:350 scale.

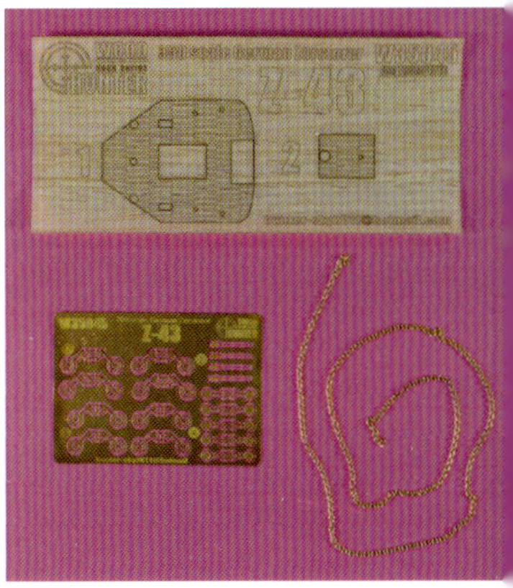

Hunter *Z43* wood deck set

Review sets courtesy of **FlyHawk Model**

ARTWOX

1:350 Scale

Similar to the Hunter offerings, this wood deck is for the Dragon *Z31* kit and has one large piece for the lower bridge deck and a smaller piece for the upper bridge deck. The sheet has duplicates of both decks allowing two kits to be upgraded; anchor chain is also included.

EDUARD

1:350 Scale

The ***Z31* etch set** is for the Dragon kit and has 74 parts on a single brass photo-etch sheet, with the deck railings all pre-cut to length. This will be an easy set to use due to the size of the parts and the slightly thicker than usual photo-etch sheet.

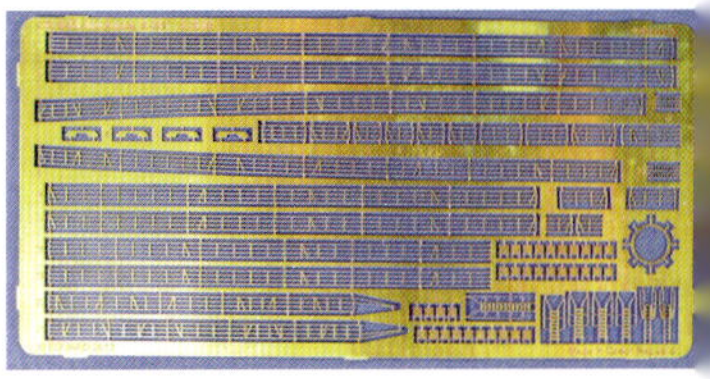

Eduard *Z31* photo-etch set

FLYHAWK

1:350 Scale

This ***Z39* detail set** contains everything needed to completely upgrade the Dragon kit: eleven photo-etch sheets with 1157 parts, two resin gun mounts, and four machined brass 5.9in gun barrels. The parts list is comprehensive, right down to a name-plate. The replacement decks all feature textured anti-skid surfaces and planking on the bridge decks and are fitted with cut-outs to fit over existing deck detail. The resin gun mounts fit inside the kit single 5.9in mounts; the brass barrels are tapered and have drilled out muzzles. There is plenty of relief etching throughout this high-quality set and most modellers will find it easy to work with given the large size of the parts in this scale; three double sided colour pages give precise folding and assembly instructions with references to kit parts.

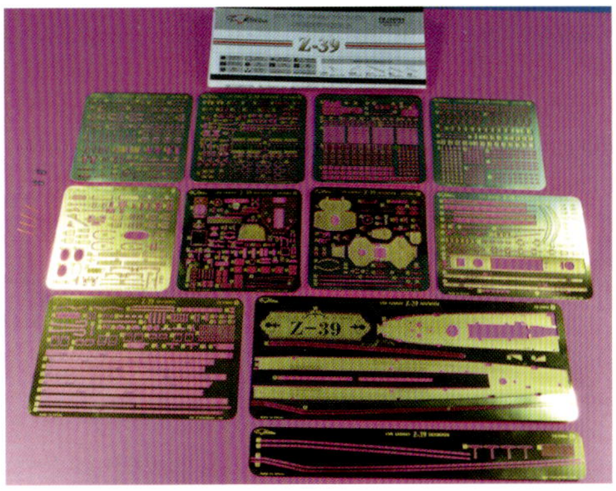

FlyHawk *Z39* detail set contents

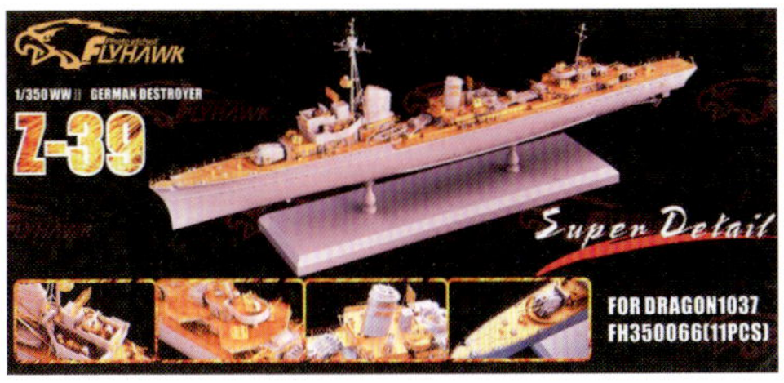

FlyHawk *Z39* detail set box

Review set courtesy of **FlyHawk Model**

Modelmakers' Showcase

IRON SHIPWRIGHT/TRUMPETER **NARVIK HARBOUR,** 9 APRIL 1940 1:350 scale

By STEIN GILDBERG

The diorama depicts the scene about 30 minutes after the initial landings at the Postal Pier. *Z11 (Bernd von Arnim)* is alongside the pier with her forward torpedo tubes and after gun mounts swung out having just sunk the Norwegian coastal defence ship *Norge* with a salvo of seven torpedoes after a spirited exchange of gunfire. Historically at this time *Z2 (George Thiele)* was at the pier, but in its place Stein elected instead to model *Z21 (Wilhelm Heidkamp)* coming alongside in order to more clearly show the differences between classes.

At the head of the pier, Generalmajor Dietl and his Chief of Staff can be seen commandeering a taxi that they used as a

transport to Narvik town. They had come ashore via ship's boat from *Z21*; the boat is moored to the pier in front of *Z21*. Most of the troops have left for Narvik while crew and soldiers are unloading supplies and clearing the decks (and taking pictures too!)

Z11 is from the Iron Shipwright resin Type 1934A kit. The underwater portion of the hull was cut away and the kit heavily modified with all platforms and the entire bridge rebuilt. The guns, boats, torpedo tubes, and deck fittings were either from Trumpeter spares or were scratch-built. The masts are brass tubing, rigging from stretched sprue, and the photo-etch from the spares box.

Z21 is from a Trumpeter 1936A kit, shortened at the stern by 10mm to conform to the dimensions of a Type 1936. As with *Z11*, the underwater portion of the hull was cut away, the masts are from brass tubing, the rigging from stretched sprue, and the photo-etch from spares.

The buildings and pier were scratch-built from wood and plastic sheet, with roofs made from sandpaper. The personnel are from North Star Models, the water from plaster and acrylics.

MODELBAU ANDREAS LASSEK *Z11 BERND VON ARNIM*

1:100 scale

By STEIN GILDBERG

This is a limited run, multi-media kit with a fibreglass hull, resin decks, and resin and metal fittings; all the components are of high quality. Good plan and profile drawings are also included but some details are not shown or are incorrect; the biggest challenge was to find additional photos and drawings for those areas.

Stein was able to add considerable extra detail using styrene, sprue, brass rod, and spare photo-etch. Extra bridge details include the doors, a chart table, speaking tubes, wiring, bridge wing supports, and a target designator sight to the rear of the rangefinder. The main gun mounts were made of brass folded to shape and then soldered. Each of the 37mm guns has over 60 scratch-built parts. The boats stowed at the forecastle break were identical in the kit but in actuality they were different; the port side boat had to be extensively modified. All the supports for the boats were made from styrene sheet, pear wood, and wire mesh.

The torpedo tubes were also heavily detailed and the torpedo loading gear was added; one of the tubes was also drilled out at the rear. The torpedo was made from a solid piece of sprue, carved and sanded to shape.

The hull openings (hull and superstructure portholes, hawse holes, recesses for the anchors, and bridge windows) were only represented by slight depressions in the kit

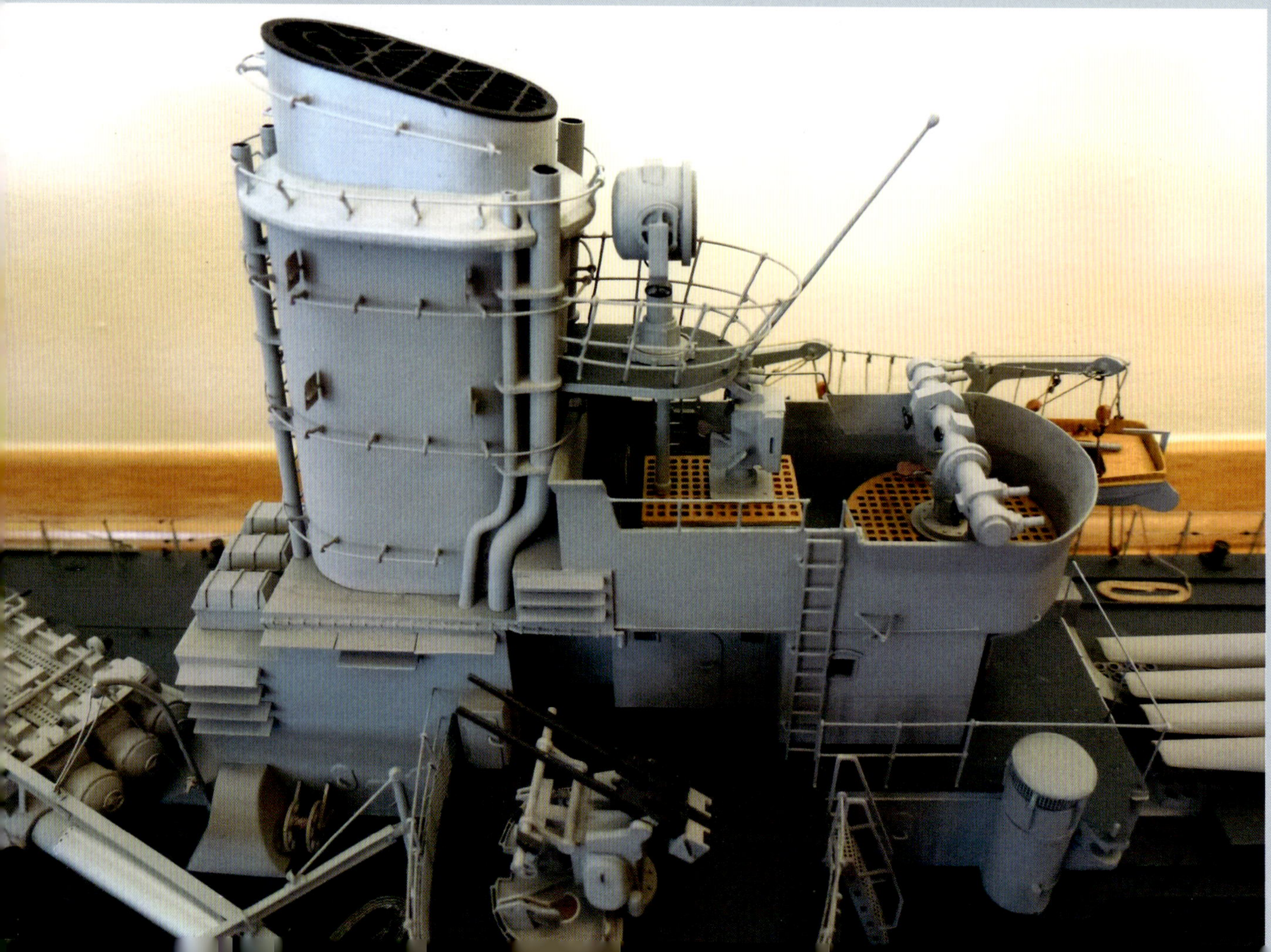

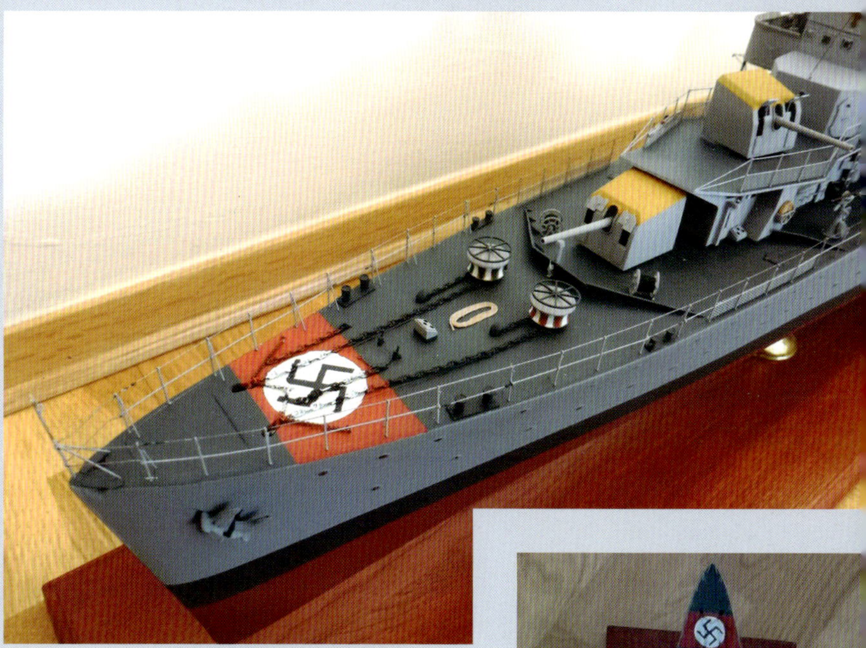

parts. These were all drilled out and shaped accordingly. The rims of the portholes are made from aluminum tube; the porthole glass was made from clear plastic tubing. The glass in the bridge windows is from Kristal Klear.

The deck planking is made from 0.8mm wood strips. The rigging is thread normally used for sailing ships, the insulators are wooden blocks made from pear wood.

CLASSIC WARSHIPS *Z1 LEBERECHT MAASS*

1:700 scale

By NORBERT THIEL

This was one of Norbert's first resin ship models and he really liked the kit. He added some extra details including the propeller guards, rigging, and photo-etch railing.

TRUMPETER *Z19 HERMANN KÜNNE*

1:350 scale

By STEIN GILDBERG

This is a much-modified Trumpeter *Z43* kit. The bow, stern, superstructure, and bridge were all extensively modified to depict this Type 1936 destroyer. The colours are from the White Ensign range, as is most of the photo-etch. *Z19* was scuttled by its own crew during the Second Battle of Narvik on 13 April 1940; its remains are still visible today.

TRUMPETER *Z28* 1:700 scale

By MATTHIAS POHL

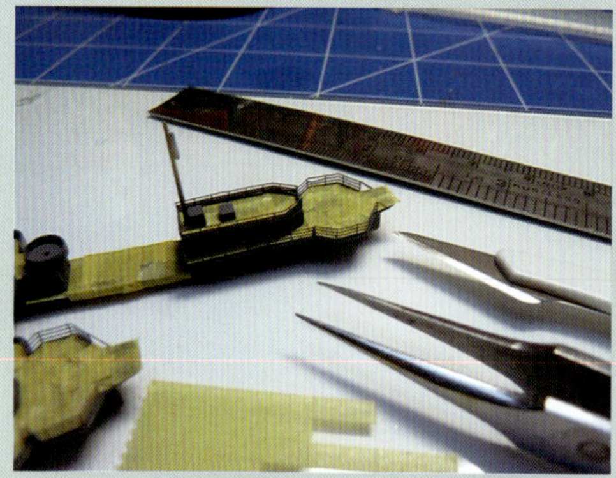

Matthias Pohl writes:
This kit of the destroyer leader *Z28* was built mostly straight out of the box, with some minor conversions to match the time period in summer 1942 when this camouflage pattern was worn. The photo-etch railings are from FlyHawk, sailors from Eduard, and I used Uschi 0.01mm thread for rigging. The fjord rocks are made of plaster and the water is made from acrylic gel. The little motor-sailer is part of a Black Dog kit. The whole scene was placed in a dust proof box from Trumpeter.

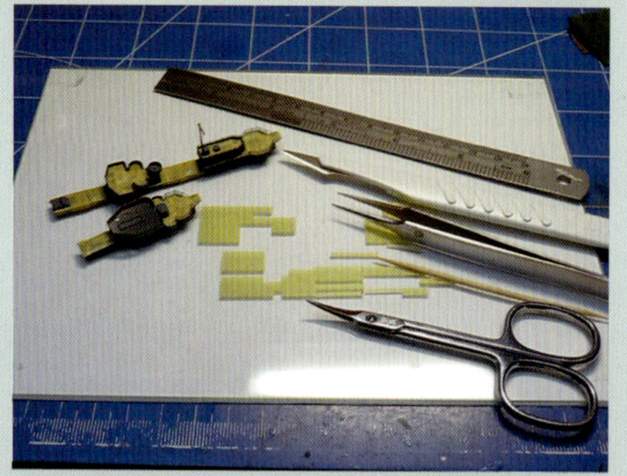

TRUMPETER *Z24* 1:700 scale

By MATTHIAS POHL

Matthias Pohl writes:
This is my version of the DKM destroyer *Z24*, a 1936A class boat, on which my father Kurt F Pohl served during the commissioning. I used the Trumpeter *Z30* kit and as I wanted to show *Z24* at the time my father did his service as a torpedo mechanic on it, the model has no traces of wear.

I used brass barrels from Master, anchor chains by FlyHawk, wooden deck by Artwox (adapted from their *Z28* deck), AA weapons from 3D-Models, railings by Saemann, and Uschi's 0.01mm flexible rigging thread.

The main guns were painted using the drawings in Eric Leon and John Asmussen's *German Naval Camouflage Vol 2* as a reference, which agrees completely with my father's recollections. I used Model Master and Vallejo colours.

Ralf Hartmann did the base and Christoph Mentzel was very helpful with the plate (thanks to both!). The left badge is a copy of the original *Zerstörerkriegsabzeichen*, which means 'destroyer war badge' and is half the size of the original. The right symbol is an original from the epaulet of my father, the career insignia of the torpedo mechanics.

TRUMPETER *Z30* 1:350 scale

By CHRIS FLODBERG

Chris Foldberg writes:
The model was built more or less straight out of the box, using the kit's photo-etch and some scraps from my spares box. The water base is complex, consisting of carved styrofoam covered in paper and then painted. Cotton and acrylic gloss varnish were used to create the white-water effects.

TRUMPETER *Z30* 1:350 scale

By SANTIAGO EZCURRA

Santiago Ezcurra writes:
This is an excellent kit, with well detailed parts that fit perfectly, crisp moulding, clear and precise instructions, a photo-etch set with radars, funnel caps, rails, and cable reels, and a full colour painting guide. I built it mostly out of the box and it took about a month to complete. I used photo-etch Lion Roar railings instead of the ones supplied with the kit as they look more appropriate.

I used Humbrol enamels to paint the upper hull and superstructure: Dark Grey (125), Ghost Grey (127), and Matt White (34). Matt Reddish Brown (37) from Revell was used for the lower hull. I weathered the model using oil paints.

DRAGON *Z37* 1:700 scale

By KATARZYNA MANIKOWSKA

This model shows *Z37* awaiting a tow after her collision with *Z32* on 30 January 1944 while on exercises in the Bay of Biscay. *Z37* was badly damaged by the impact, a torpedo warhead exploded and a severe fire broke out amidships. She was successfully towed to Bordeaux but never returned to service.

The model was built mostly from the box with the necessary modifications to show the damage that resulted from the collision and subsequent fire. Most of the photo-etch came from the set included in the kit, but some small brackets and the photo-etch railings were added.

DRAGON *Z31* 1:350 scale

By ULF LUNDBERG

The model was built mostly out of the box, with railings from Eduard and paravanes from l'Arsenal. The masts were scratch-built from piano wire and copper tubing, with rigging of fly-tying line. It was painted with airbrush artists paints from Schmincke-Aerocolor.

TRUMPETER *Z25* 1:350 scale

By MATHIAS CARL

Mathias Carl writes:
I've built *Z25* as it appeared in 1945 at Wilhelmshaven. At that time *Z25* had the new 37mm Flak M42 L/69 mounts so I scratch-built those using barrels from MasterModels. Other scratch-built details include the bridge equipment, the clear plexiglass covers above the torpedo tubes, ventilation vents, FuMO radar, fire hoses, and the mines seen on the after deck as the kit supplied ones were too small. The wood deck was printed on my inkjet printer. The photo-etched railings, ladders, cable reels, etc are from different generic White Ensign sets.

The model was brush painted using Revell Aqua Colours which are good matches for German warships. The rigging is made from stretched sprue.

TRUMPETER *Z43* 1:350 scale

By NORBERT THIEL

Norbert Thiel writes:

I like to have my models waterlined in a seascape so I cut the lower hull away using tape to mark the cut line and then cutting using a small razor saw. The model is largely built straight from the box, with some extra detailing. The foot rails on the funnels are made from railing cut to single bar and then adjusted to the shape of the funnel. The gun barrels are from Master, crew figures from Pit-Road's German sailors, the round life-buoys from NNT, and flags from HP models. I used wire to add extra detail to the life rafts; rigging is stretched sprue.

The model was airbrushed using Tamiya colours, with detail painting done with Humbrol, Revell, or Agama colours. The base is made from 'Liquid Water' carved into a sea-like appearance and then painted in dark blue. When that dried, I added three to five layers of clear gloss and highlights in matt white.

Z2 Georg Thiele (Type 1934) 1938
Standard pre-war scheme worn by all Type 1934, Type 1934A, and Type 1936

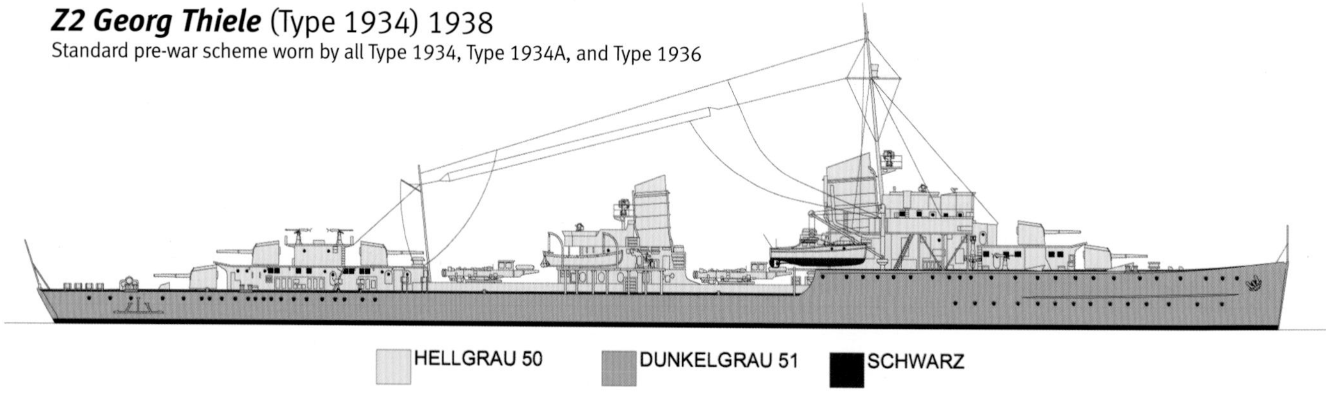

Z5 Paul Jacobi (Type 1934A) 1943

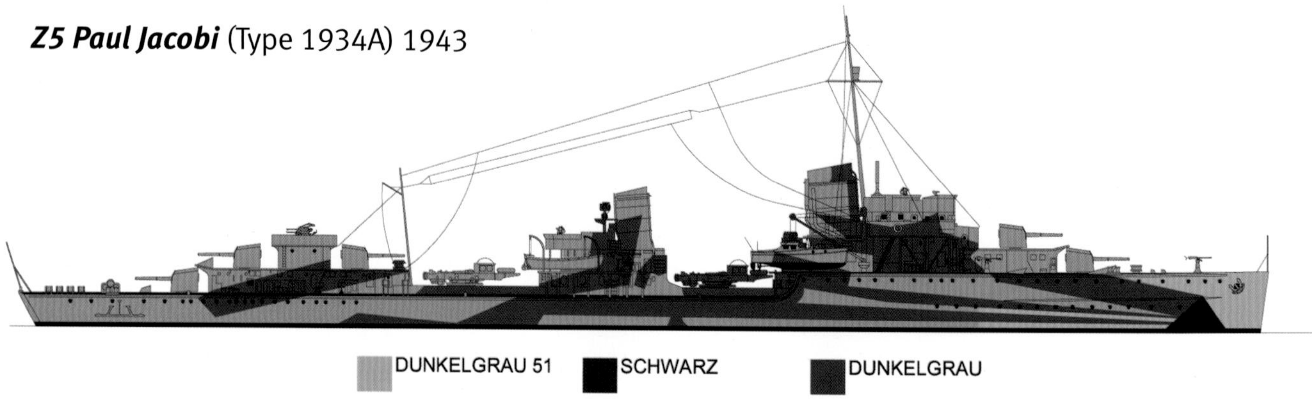

Z5 Paul Jacobi (Type 1934A) 1945
High boot-topping, also worn by *Z29* (1945)

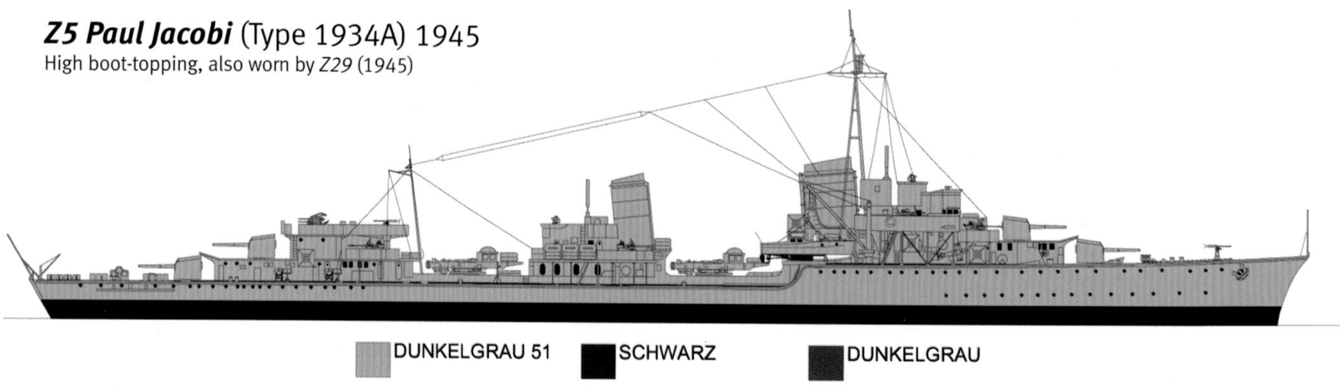

Z6 Theodor Riedel (Type 1934A) 1942
Vanishing point scheme

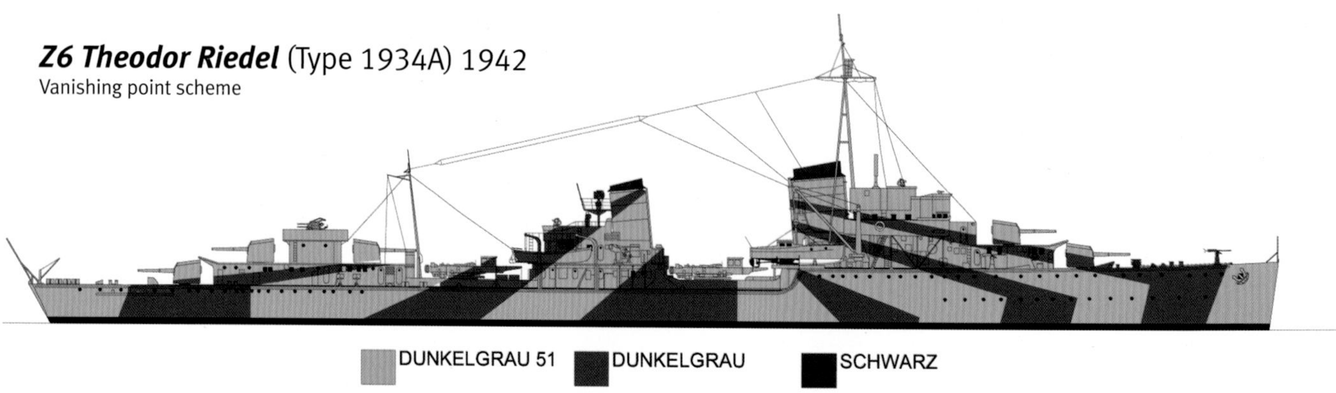

Z6 Theodor Riedel (Type 1934A) 1944
Pre-war scheme with white panels at bow and stern

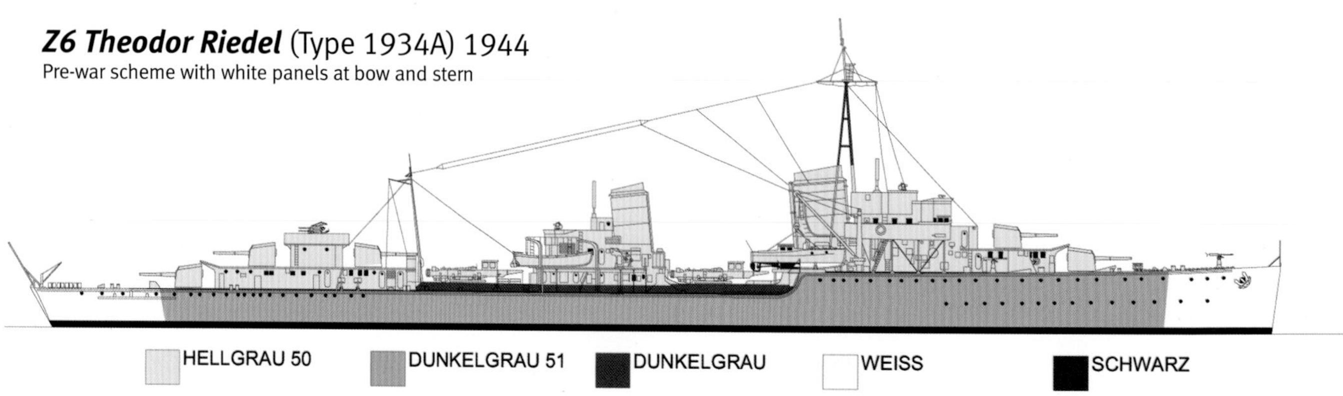

Z14 Friedrich Ihn (Type 1934A) 1941

Retained scheme after 1941 refit with tripod mast and radar

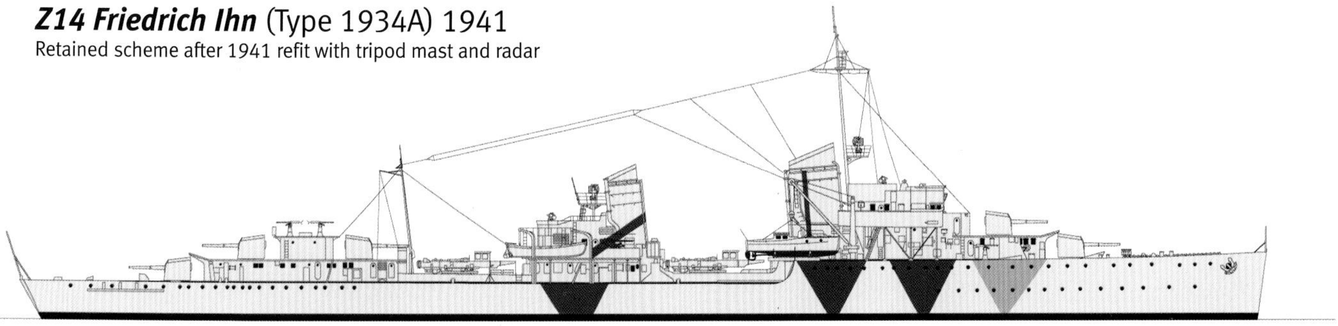

HELLGRAU 50 · DUNKELGRAU 51 · DUNKELGRAU · SCHWARZ

Z23 (Type 1936A) 1940

Light grey hull and superstructure, also worn by *Z24* (1941)

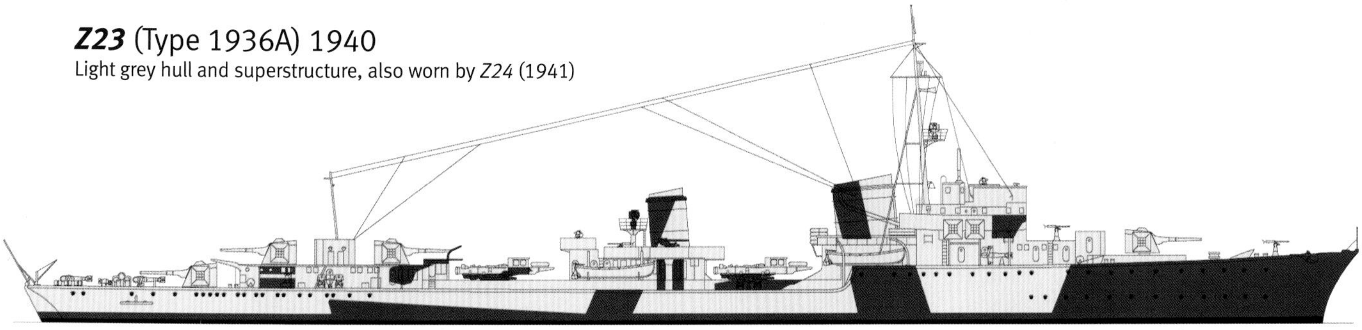

HELLGRAU 50 · DUNKELGRAU 51 · SCHWARZ · DUNKELGRAU

Z23 (Type 1936A) 1941

Dark grey hull and superstructure

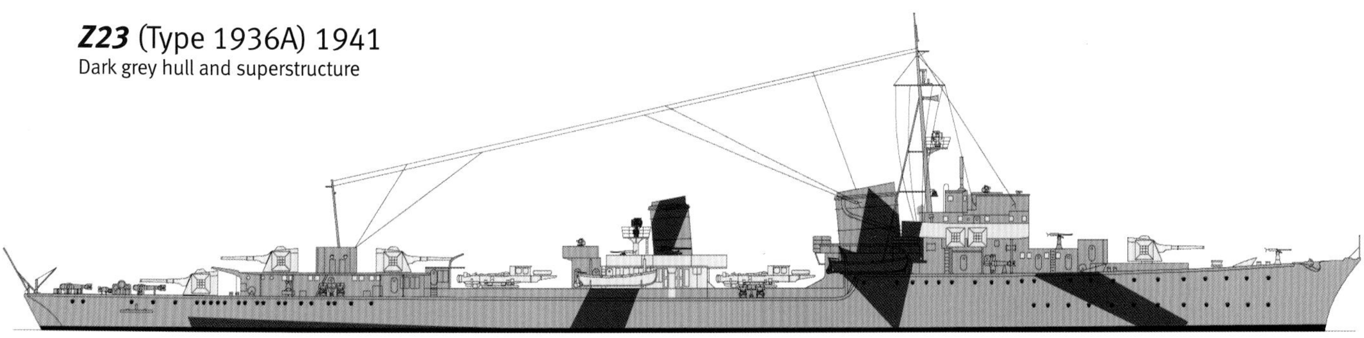

HELLGRAU 50 · DUNKELGRAU 51 · SCHWARZ · DUNKELGRAU

Z26 (Type 1936A) 1941

Standard scheme also worn by *Z25* (1941), *Z27* (1942), *Z29* (1942) and with slight variations by *Z4* (1941), *Z6* (1941)

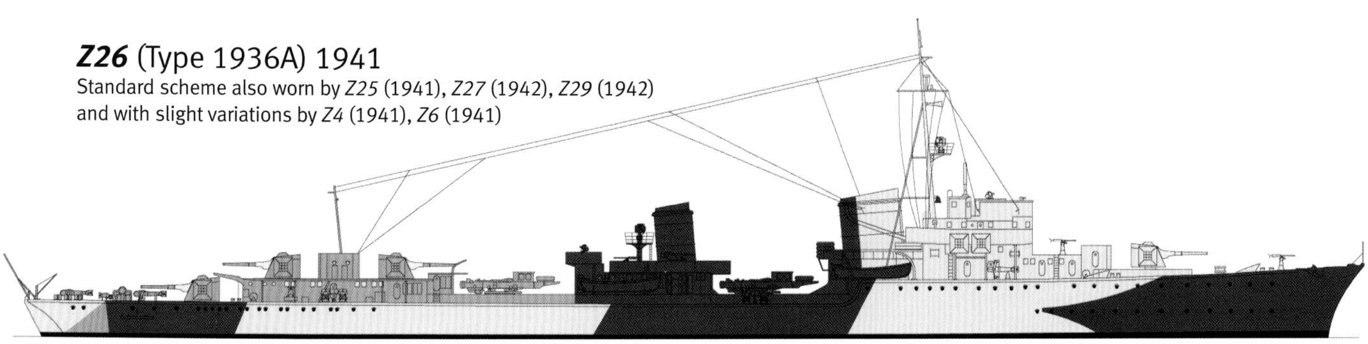

HELLGRAU 50 · DUNKELGRAU 51 · SCHWARZ · DUNKELGRAU

Z30 (Type 1936A) 1942

On the port side, there is no white bow panel; a full bow wave extends from the bow to the white panel under the bridge.

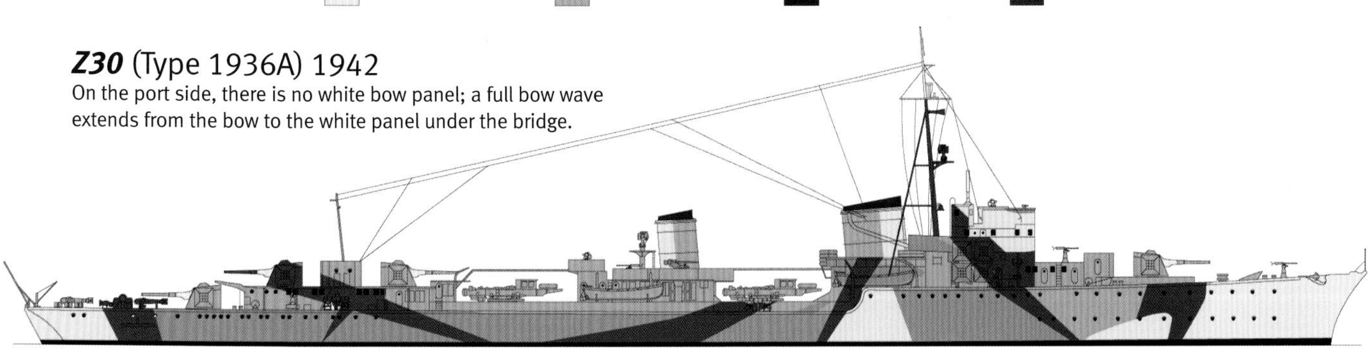

DUNKELGRAU 51 · SCHWARZ · DUNKELGRAU · WEISS

Z32 (Type 1936A Mob) 1943

Vanishing point scheme also worn by *Z33* (1943)

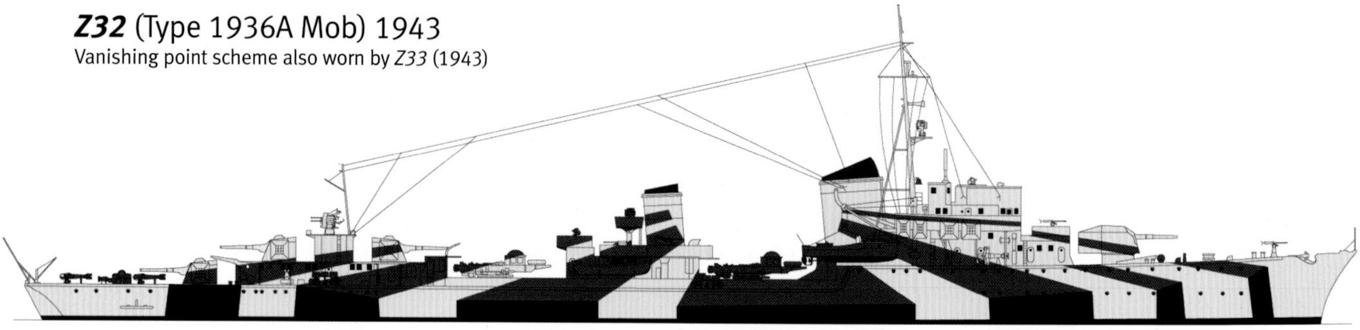

HELLGRAU 50 DUNKELGRAU 51 SCHWARZ DUNKELGRAU

Z33 (Type 1936A Mob) 1944

Overall dark grey

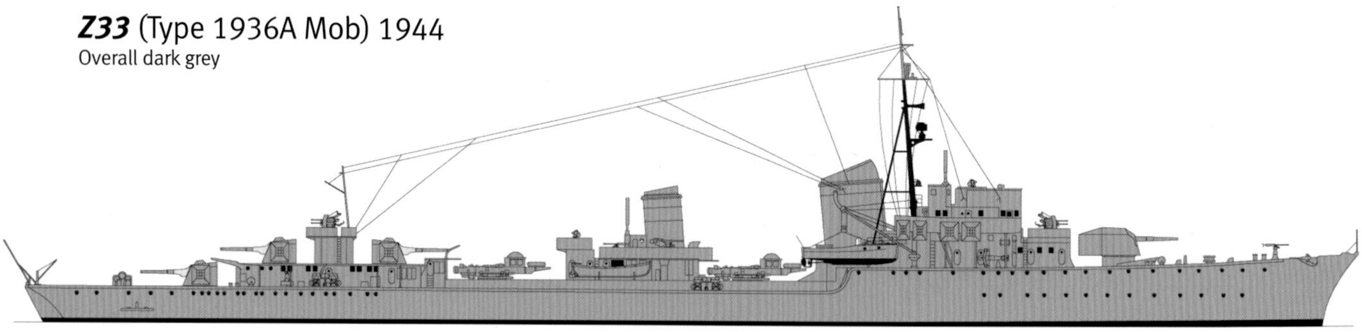

DUNKELGRAU 51 SCHWARZ

Z37 (Type 1936A Mob) 1943

Vanishing point scheme

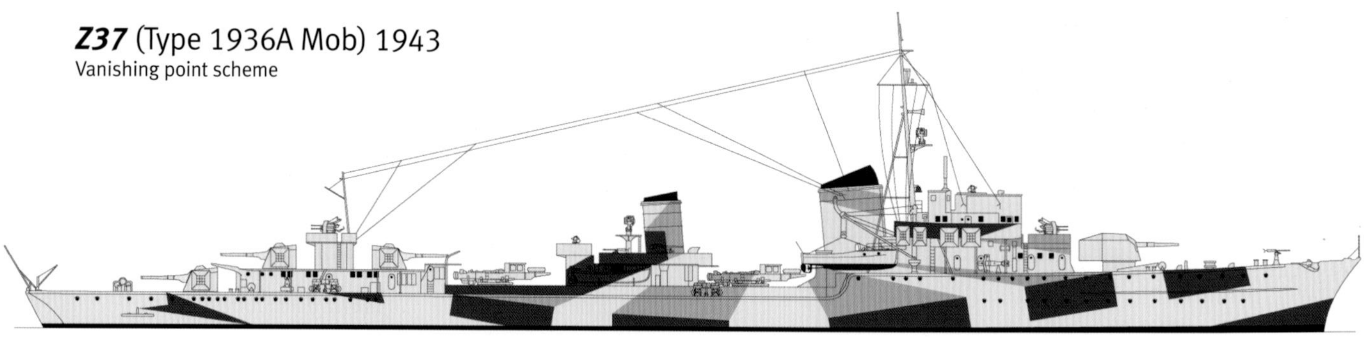

HELLGRAU 50 DUNKELGRAU 51 SCHWARZ DUNKELGRAU

Z39 (Type 1936A Mob) 1944

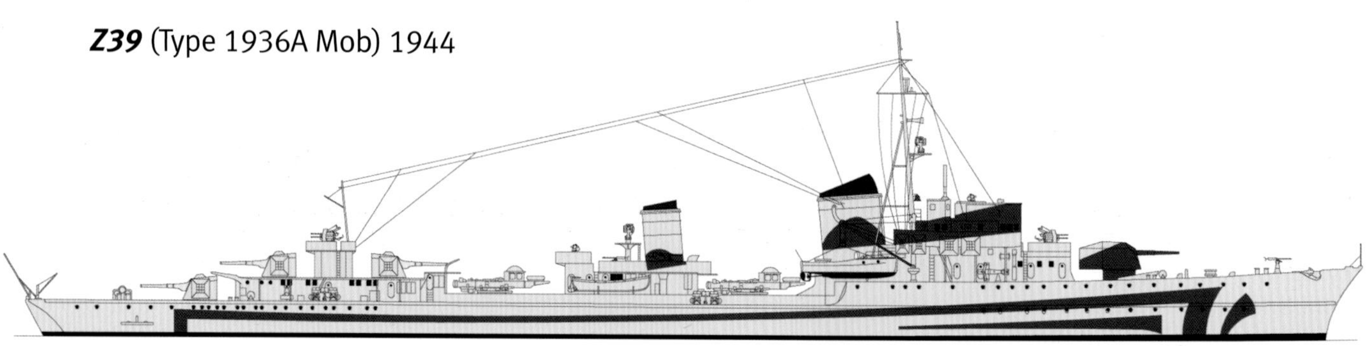

DUNKELGRAU 51 SCHWARZ DUNKELGRAU

Colour Key:

Dunkelgrau	Dark Grey
Dunkelgrau 51	Dark Grey with blue tone
Hellgrau 50	Light Grey with blue tone
Schwarz	Black
Weiss	White

Appearance

CAMOUFLAGE AND PAINT SCHEMES

The standard pre-war scheme was dark grey hull, light grey superstructure, dark grey foremast above the funnel, and tactical numbers in white (there was no standard typeface). Funnel cowls were silver or black, with some ships switching from one colour to the other. The eagle and swastika emblem on the front of the bridge was cast bronze. It was removed from most ships at the outbreak of war, but some carried it into 1941 – ships completed after September 1939 were not fitted with it. A metal name plate was fitted at the top of the hull aft close to the propeller guards.

Camouflage patterns made their first appearance during the Norwegian campaign in 1940; see the drawings section for a selection of schemes. Not all the ships were camouflaged but were painted overall light grey or dark grey or in the peacetime scheme; new construction was usually light grey overall. Some ships with camouflage patterns stationed in Norway in 1942–43 used a dark grey wash overall which left the pattern still visible underneath.

The metal decks were either dark grey (*Dunkelgrau*) or black; camouflage did not extend onto the decks. Wooden bridge decks were unpainted. When not painted, life rafts were khaki in colour. Camouflage patterns were frequently carried over the rafts.

Aircraft Recognition Markings.
Coloured gun mounts:
Yellow – Norwegian operations including April 1940.
Red – Destroyers based in France; the gun mounts were often covered in canvas when in port.
Blue – Operation Cerberus in February 1942.
It was the commander's discretion whether the entire gun mount or just the top was painted.

Deck markings:
Swastikas in a white circle forward and aft. The forward position varied from just ahead of the capstans to just behind the hawse-holes; the aft position was behind the propeller guards. A red surrounding band was sometimes applied extending to the deck edge. Removable fabric markings were also used.

The first use of the deck markings was during the Norwegian operation in April 1940.

Z8 Bruno Heinemann wearing camouflage while stationed in France in 1941. She has been modified for FuMO 21 with the reconfigured bridge and the removal of the forward searchlight; the radar array has been deleted by the censor. The foremast is now a tripod, both funnels have been shortened, and there are no weather shields on the torpedo tubes. The vessel in the foreground is either *Z23* or *Z24*.

BARBARA UPGRADE

In November 1944 plans code named 'Barbara' were drawn up to substantially increase the AA capability of the destroyer fleet. Each class had a specific upgrade scheme, but all involved replacing the foremost gun on the after gun deck with additional AA platforms.

Type 1934/1934A: Six twin 37mm (two ahead of the bridge, two on the AA deck, two replacing No 3 gun), one single 20mm bow chaser, two twin 20mm in the bridge wings, one quad 20mm aft.

Type 1936 / 1936A / Type 1936A (Mob):

Left: *Z24* in dazzle camouflage while operating in the Bay of Biscay in 1941. Items of interest are the lighter bow panel, single 5.9in mount forward with rafts on the top and sides, degaussing cable running along the top edge of the hull from just aft of the anchors to the stern, and the FuMO 21 radar array.

Z32 in 1943 at Bordeaux, sporting her 'vanishing point' scheme; note how it is carried over the life rafts. The canvas patch on the bridge wing is the cover for her tactical number. A degaussing cable is fitted along the top of the hull, both searchlights are fitted and she is carrying the port side cutter; no derrick is fitted.

Six twin 37mm (two ahead of the bridge, two amidships on the AA deck, two replacing No 2 gun – No 3 gun in Type 1936), two single 37mm amidships on the AA deck, three twin 20mm (one bow chaser, two in the bridge wings), one quad 20mm aft, and four AA rocket launchers.

***Z28*:** Seven twin 37mm (two ahead of the bridge, four amidships on the AA deck, one on the after deckhouse), five twin 20mm (one bow chaser, two in the bridge wings, two on the after deckhouse); she would retain all her main gun mounts.

Type 1936B (Mob): Seven twin 37mm (two ahead of the bridge, two amidships on the AA deck, three replacing No 3 gun), two single 37mm replacing bridge quad 20mm, one twin 20mm bow chaser, one quad 20mm aft, and AA rocket launchers.

Only *Z5*, *Z10*, *Z15*, *Z25*, *Z29*, and *Z39* received the full 'Barbara' upgrade; *Z29*'s upgrade was in progress when the war ended.

CLASS VARIATIONS AND MODIFICATIONS

The destroyers underwent constant upgrades throughout their service lives; imprecise dates, conflicting sources, and scant photographic evidence are significant obstacles to compiling a definitive list of all the alterations. The following includes the known modifications with approximate time frames.

Type 1934 (*Z1–Z4*)
General Characteristics: The hull had a straight stem and raked transom stern. The forecastle featured very little upward sheer or outward flare, although it did have a slight radiused deckedge. The upper bridge had a rounded face. In order to accommodate the starboard cutter amidships, the AA deck was asymmetrical with the starboard side slightly ahead of the port. They were fitted with a single rudder. The mainmast was on the forward end of the after shelter deck immediately in front of No 3 gun.

AA Fit: Two twin 37mm mounts on the AA deck; the port side mount was aft of the starboard mount due to the asymmetrical deck. Six single 20mm: two on the forecastle abreast No 2 gun, two on the forecastle forward of the boat derricks, and two atop the after deckhouse.

Boats: One motor boat to port and one to starboard on the forecastle beside the forward funnel with derricks fitted just forward. One cutter on davits fitted to starboard abaft the AA deck. A small dinghy was stowed to port abaft the after funnel.

Identification Features: Very tall fore funnel, mainmast in front of No 3 gun, two 5in mounts forward, large propeller guards, pre-war tactical numbers.

MODIFICATIONS
Pre-War: All four ships had the stemhead

TACTICAL NUMBERS

Pre-war the destroyers were organized into three-ship divisions; flotillas comprised two divisions. Each ship displayed a two digit number on the hull side that denoted their division and position within that division – for example '11' denotes first division, first ship; '13' denotes first division, third ship; '41' denotes fourth division, first ship. When the position number changed, or a destroyer shifted to another division, the tactical number was also changed so some ships carried more than one number during their service. The tactical numbers were painted out on the outbreak of war in 1939.

As overall flagship (Flag Officer Torpedo Boats), *Z1* did not wear any tactical number. *Z10* was part of Division 6 before moving to Division 8.

Ship	Flotilla	Division	Tactical Number(s)	Ship	Flotilla	Division	Tactical Number(s)
Z1				Z12	4	8	82
Z2	1	1	13	Z13	4	8	83
Z3	1	1	12	Z14	1	3	31, 32, 33
Z4	1	1	11	Z15	1	3	31, 32, 33
Z5	2	2	21	Z16	1	3	31, 32, 33
Z6	2	2	22	Z17	3	5	51
Z7	2	2	23	Z18	3	5	53
Z8	4	6	61, 63	Z19	3	5	52
Z9	4	6	61, 62, 63	Z20	2	4	42
Z10	4	6 & 8	61, 62, 81	Z21	2	4	43
Z11	4	6	62	Z22	2	4	41

Z2 Georg Thiele with enlarged bridge and spray strake fitted; the forecastle has not yet been modified. The spray strake was removed when the forecastle was raised, suggesting that it was an experimental measure only. Other items of interest are the dark colour of the foremast above the funnel, crowsnest located above the crosstrees on the foremast, and the foremast searchlight enclosed with a canvas screen. *(US National Archives 80-G-15663 via Roger Torgeson)*

raised by 20in and lengthened by 3ft, resulting in a raked bow; the upper bridge was enlarged and fitted with a square front. The decks and inner bottoms were strengthened and the anti-roll equipment removed and replaced with bilge keels. *Z2* had a horizontal spray strake fitted at the main deck level under the forecastle, running from just aft of the anchors to No 2 gun; it was removed prior to the war.

Summer 1940: *Z4* fitted with non-rotatable FuMO 21 radar: foremast searchlight and TAM removed, radar office with radar array on top fitted at rear of bridge, bridge rangefinder fitted in its own tub and repositioned immediately in front of the radar office. Propeller guards repositioned higher on hull, degaussing cable fitted along the top of the hull.

By Feb 1942: *Z4* fitted with tripod foremast and one quad 20mm atop the after deckhouse. Single 20mm re-arranged: one under the barrel of No 2 gun, two on the forecastle abreast No 2 gun, two in the bridge wings, one under the barrel of No 4 gun.

Unidentified Type 1934 showing the radiused deckedge – in effect, a slight turtleback – to the forecastle and the rounded front to the upper bridge. *(Author's collection)*

Z10 Hans Lody when based in France between September and November 1940. The funnels have not yet been cut down but there is a deck-edge degaussing cable; the after funnel has a canvas cap. The depth charge throwers can be seen at the deck edge below the after deckhouse and both single 20mm are visible behind a canvas screen atop the after deckhouse. Note the angled flange around the after rangefinder tub, the two crew members in the rubber raft, and that the gun shields are a different colour from the hull and superstructure. *(Author's collection)*

Z17 Diether von Roeder in Narvik harbor on 11 April 1940, showing the effects of the attack the day before by the Royal Navy's 2nd Destroyer Flotilla. Note the shell holes under No 2 gun and under the forward funnel where a fire has scorched the hull plating. These hits and others further aft immobilized the destroyer; she was scuttled alongside the Postal Pier on 13 April. Also note the degaussing cable. *(US National Archives 80-G-15687 via RogerTorgeson)*

1943–1944: *Z4* forward and after funnels cut down, FuMO 21 replaced with FuMO 24/25, FuMO 63 fitted to foremast.
Aug 1944: *Z4* fitted with new bow with pronounced sheer and flare ('Atlantic bow').

Notes: As completed the ships were tender – quick to roll and recover; a serious detriment for a stable gun platform. The forecastle modifications did not improve their seaworthiness. With a following sea they steered very badly, tending to turn broadside and requiring considerable helmsman effort and the use of engines to return to course. To ensure stability, fuel oil levels were not allowed to fall below 30 per cent remaining, which considerably reduced their range. Hull flexing problems reduced the mine load to 42 by 1944. They were such a disappointment in service that plans were made prior to the outbreak of war to reduce them to a training role by 1941; by May 1940 only *Z4* was still afloat.

Type 1934A (*Z5–Z16*)

General Characteristics: Before the first Type 1934 had been launched, doubts were being expressed about their sea-keeping abilities. Accordingly, the forecastle was redesigned for this class with more outward flare. The fuel capacity was reduced, probably in an attempt to improve stability. With a view to improving steering characteristics, they were fitted with twin rudders. In all

Two Type 1934/1934A destroyers in line ahead on the starboard quarter of a light cruiser. Both ships have their amidships cutter swung out. Note the very large propeller guards.

other respects these ships were identical to the Type 1934.

AA Fit and Boats: As Type 1934
Individual Differences:
Z5–Z7 completed with the round front to the upper bridge; the rest had the enlarged bridge with square front.
Z8 completed with the prototype 5.9in guns in No 1, No 2, No 3, and No 5 positions; after trials, she was fitted with the standard 5in mounts.
Z5–Z8 (Deschimag-built) had six narrow diameter pipes at the rear of the forward funnel and a square cut at the bottom of the side plating connecting the forecastle to the main deck.
Z9–Z13 (Germania-built) had two wide diameter pipes with three narrower pipes between at the rear of the forward funnel; the centre bridge window was slightly raised above the other four.
Z5–Z13 had two large diameter pipes on the front of the after funnel.
Z14–Z16 had two large diameter pipes with four thinner pipes between on the front of the after funnel.
Z14-Z16 completed with raked bows.

Identification Features: As Type 1934

MODIFICATIONS
Pre-war: *Z5–Z7* fitted with enlarged upper bridge and raked bow.
By 1940: *Z8–Z13* fitted with raked bow.
By Apr 1940: *Z5* port side derrick removed.
1940–1941: *Z5, Z6, Z7, Z8, Z10, Z14, Z15, Z16* fitted with non-rotatable FuMO 21 radar: bridge configured similar to *Z4* and foremast searchlight removed. Also fitted with degaussing cable around top of hull, tripod foremast, and propeller guards repositioned higher on hull. (*Z6* was fitted with the first FuMO 21 installation by Apr 1940).
1941–1942: *Z5, Z6, Z10, Z12, Z14, Z15* funnels cut down; *Z5, Z6, Z10, Z14, Z15, Z16* fitted with one quad 20mm on top of after deckhouse. *Z5, Z10, Z15* fitted with weather shields on the torpedo tubes.
1943–1944: *Z10* fitted with a horizontal spray strake at the main deck level under the forecastle, running from just aft of the anchors to No 2 gun.
By late 1944: *Z5, Z6, Z10, Z14, Z15* FuMO 21 replaced with FuMO 24/25, searchlight on after funnel replaced with FuMO 63, FuMB Metox also fitted; *Z6* fitted with additional FuMO 63 on foremast; *Z5, Z10, Z15* fitted with goalpost foremast; *Z5, Z15* fitted with Atlantic bow; *Z5, Z10, Z15* 'Barbara' AA upgrade completed; *Z14* removal of No 3 gun for increased AA.

AA fits at end of war:
Z5 – Two twin 37mm abaft No 2 gun on forecastle, two twin 37mm on AA deck, two single 37mm abreast the former No 3 gun. Two twin 20mm on forecastle either side of the bridge, two twin 20mm in bridge wings, one quad 20mm and one single 20mm on extended after deckhouse.
Z10 – Two twin 37mm abaft No 2 gun on forecastle, two twin 37mm on AA deck, two twin 37mm abreast the former No 3 gun. One twin 20mm on forecastle, two twin 20mm in bridge wings, one twin 20mm in place of No 3 gun, one quad 20mm and one single 20mm on extended after deckhouse.
Z14 – Two twin 37mm on AA deck. Two twin 20mm abreast No 2 gun on forecastle, two twin 20mm in bridge wings, two twin 20mm abreast the former No 3 gun, one quad 20mm and one twin 20mm on extended after deckhouse.
Z15 – Two twin 37mm abaft No 2 gun on forecastle, two twin 37mm on AA deck, two twin 37mm abreast the former No 3 gun, one twin 37mm on extended after deckhouse. One twin 20mm on forecastle, two twin 20mm on bridge wings, one quad 20mm on extended after deckhouse.

Notes: As with the Type 1934, these ships also proved to be a disappointment in service; the modifications to the forecastle did not improve their sea-keeping or steering abilities and they remained subject to the 30 per cent fuel load minimum. They also developed hull bending problems and their mine

Z14 Friedrich Ihn pre-war. This view shows the asymmetrical AA deck and the davits for the starboard side cutter. No mine rails are fitted on the starboard side, and the funnel has a canvas cap. The girder on the front of the after gun deck used to lift reload torpedoes is swung out and rigged to port.

There are actually three destroyers visible in this photo taken after the German surrender in 1945. In the foreground is the port side after deck of *Z15 Erich Steinbrinck* showing two of her twin 37mm and the quad 20mm clustered around the after deckhouse (the shield is folded back on the quad 20mm). Behind is the bridge of *Z5 Paul Jacobi* showing the *tormast* fitted to enable the FuMO 24/25 to rotate. Behind is *Z6 Theodor Riedel* with the FuMO 63 fitted to her foremast. Note the White Ensign!

carrying capacity was similarly reduced.

Type 1936 (*Z17–Z22*)

General Characteristics: A major effort to improve the sea-keeping qualities was made with this class. Topweight was reduced by lowering and widening the funnels and funnel cowls, and lowering the height of the superstructure around the after funnel. The deckhouse atop the after superstructure was reduced in size and its 20mm single mounts moved to the enlarged and symmetrical AA deck. The hull was lengthened forward to provide more buoyancy and the beam was increased, and all were fitted with the enlarged square-fronted bridge. The bridge rangefinder and TAM were fitted in tubs, the TAM atop a pedestal at the back of the bridge

The mainmast was moved to the top of the after deckhouse, clearing firing arcs for No 3 gun. The gun decks for No 2, No 3, and No 4 mounts were enlarged to provide more working space for the crews. The tops of the boat derricks on the forecastle were enclosed within enlarged bridge wings. The foremast searchlight position was adjustable from just above the TAM to halfway up the mast.

Below the waterline, the deflector wedge and the centreline skeg were reduced in size in an effort to improve the steering characteristics.

AA Fit: Two twin 37mm mounts on the AA deck. Six single 20mm: one at the bow, two on the forecastle abreast No 2 gun, two on the AA deck, one under the barrel of No 4 gun.

Boats: One motor boat to port and one to starboard on the forecastle beside the forward funnel with derricks fitted just forward. One cutter on davits fitted to starboard and one to port abaft the AA deck.

Individual Differences: *Z20–Z22* were fitted with the Atlantic bow; their anchors were carried in hawsepipes on the sides of the hull. *Z21* had the TAM fitted forward of the rangefinder not in a tub, nor on a pedestal.

Identification Features: Short wide funnels, two 5in mounts forward, mainmast atop after deckhouse, small propeller guards at the waterline, TAM on the pedestal at the rear of the bridge, pre-war tactical numbers.

MODIFICATIONS

By end 1939: Anti-roll system removed from all except *Z20*. bilge keels fitted to all.

By Mar 1940: *Z17* fitted with degaussing cable along the top of the hull

By May 1940: *Z20* fitted with thicker foremast to the level of the searchlight and bridge reconfigured similar to *Z21* with TAM moved forward of the rangefinder. Degaussing cable fitted along the top of the hull.

1941–1942: *Z20* rear of bridge enlarged and fitted with FuMO 24/25, FuMO 63 replaced the searchlight on the after funnel, FuMB Metox fitted, tripod foremast fitted, one 20mm quad fitted atop after deckhouse, mainmast moved forward of No 3 gun.

Oct 1942: *Z20* fitted with weather shields on the torpedo tubes.

1943–1944: *Z20* had 20mm singles on AA deck replaced with 37mm singles. Additional 20mm fitted: two twin 20mm abaft No 2 gun on forecastle, two twin 20mm in bridge wings, one single 20mm under No 2 gun barrel, one single 20mm under No 4 gun barrel.

Notes: The six ships were ordered in 1936 and commissioned from August 1938 to September 1939. Despite the modifications, the sea-keeping abilities of the class were not greatly improved. After April 1940 only Z20 remained afloat and she suffered from the same hull bending issues as the earlier ships.

Type 1936A (*Z23–Z30*)

General Characteristics: As a result of the mediocre sea-keeping qualities of the previous ships, an attempt was made with this class to create a destroyer that could successfully operate in the Atlantic. The ensuing design process was complicated by constantly changing specifications regarding

Z23 fitted with her twin turret forward. The number '23' (clearly visible when the photo is enlarged) on the bridge face is her wartime tactical number used for recognition when at sea; most destroyers carried them. They were on wooden boards and were covered with canvas while in port.

range, weight, speed, sea-keeping and a desire to increase the size of the main armament to 5.9in guns. In the end, both to expedite and to standardize construction, it was decided to simply repeat the Type 1936 with modifications required to fit the larger guns.

The hull was fitted with a bulbous forefoot, and the shape of the transom stern was modified to come to a point. The fuel tanks were re-arranged to be lower in the hull. The reload torpedo storage was changed to lockers fitted to the main deck, one on each side of each set of tubes. The depth charge throwers were moved abreast the after torpedo tubes, additional throwers were added abreast the forward torpedo tubes.

The TAM was removed and a radar office was fitted at the after end of the upper bridge with a FuMO 21 radar mattress on its roof, just behind the rangefinder, which was a 10ft model. The bridge was moved forward and made more compact to allow the radar array to rotate without hitting the foremast. Forward of the bridge the superstructure was reduced to a small deckhouse. The superstructure aft of the after funnel was reduced in size and the amidships AA deck was reshaped with cut-outs to accommodate the amidships boats.

With the exception of *Z28*, the mount in front of the bridge was meant to be a twin turret. It was delayed during development and all seven completed with a single mount forward. The turret was fitted retroactively to *Z23*, *Z24*, *Z25*, and *Z29*. *Z26* and *Z27* were lost still carrying the single mount forward; *Z28* was never intended to have the turret, and *Z30* was never fitted with it.

Z28 was fitted as a flagship with a large deckhouse constructed on the after superstructure to provide office and accommodation space. The displaced No 2 mount was re-positioned ahead of the bridge, above and behind No 1 mount – similar to the arrangement of the proceeding classes.

All were fitted with the Atlantic bow with anchors stowed on the main deck, a tripod foremast, and degaussing cables along the top of the hull.

AA Fit: Two twin 37mm mounts on the AA deck, six single 20mm (one at the bow, one forward of the bridge on the deckhouse, two

Z29 in Norwegian waters with her single 5.9in mount forward. She is carrying life rafts on the gun mounts, against the bridge wings, and against the after superstructure. *(Author's collection)*

on the AA deck, one under the barrel of No 3 mount and one under the barrel of No 4 mount). *Z28* single 20mm: one at the bow, one under the barrel of No 2 mount, two on the AA deck, two on the roof of the after deckhouse at the forward end.

Boats: For all but *Z28*, one motor boat to port on the forecastle beside the forward funnel with a derrick fitted just forward. One cutter on davits to starboard on the forecastle beside the forward funnel; the derrick forward was not fitted. One cutter on davits fitted to starboard and one to port partially under the AA deck. *Z28* retained the same layout as the Type 1936 with two motorboats and derricks on the forecastle; the two cutters amidships were under the AA deck.
Individual Differences: *Z28* had a large deckhouse on the after superstructure and two single 5.9in mounts forward of the bridge. An emblem of a black panther in flight with a rolled umbrella was on the bridge face. *Z30* was fitted with catwalks over the torpedo tubes and had a four-leaf clover emblem on the bridge face.
Identification Features: Short wide funnels, mainmast atop after deckhouse, small propeller guards halfway up the hull, port side derrick and starboard side davits on forecastle, single mount forward (turret or single gun). *Z28* large after deckhouse and two single mounts forward.

MODIFICATIONS
No known upgrades: *Z26*
1942: *Z28* mainmast shifted forward of after deckhouse and one 20mm quad fitted on after deckhouse.
By May 1942: *Z27* fitted with one quad 20mm on after deckhouse and one quad 20mm in front of bridge.

What appears to be a minor collision between an unidentified Type 1936A (Mob) and another warship with the crews of both ships expressing some concern. Note the mine rails, canvas covered winch and paravane crane, pointed stern, and the plaques on the gun shields.

Z27 with the single 5.9in mount forward and quad 20mm forward of the bridge and on the after deckhouse. Her covered tactical number board can be seen on the front of the bridge. The FuMO 21 above the bridge has been blanked out by the censor. Note the rafts stacked against the after funnel.

Amidships detail of *Z39* fitting out in the summer of 1943. A torpedo is being hoisted using the block and tackle and boom attached to the girder at the front of the AA deck. Note the curved cowl on the forward funnel, the boiler room intake louvres, funnel handrails, the open torpedo control position, and the starboard reload girder; funnel cowls are silver.

Aug 1942: *Z23* fitted with twin turret
Nov 1942: *Z25* fitted with twin turret
1942–1943: *Z23*, *Z24*, *Z25*, *Z27*, *Z28*, *Z29* fitted with weather shields on the torpedo tubes.
Jan 1943: *Z24* fitted with twin turret
1943–1944: *Z23*, *Z24* fitted with one quad 20mm on after deckhouse and one quad 20mm in front of bridge; *Z24* fitted with two quad 20mm on AA deck in place of 20mm singles; *Z23*, *Z24*, *Z25*, *Z30* FuMO 21 replaced with FuMO 24/25, FuMB Metox also fitted; *Z25* fitted with FuMB 6 Palau on foremast and FuMB Bali at the masthead. *Z24* fitted with spray strake from the anchors to the forecastle break, *Z28* fitted with spray strake forward.
By late 1944: *Z25* 'Barbara' AA upgrade completed.
Dec 1944: *Z29* 'Barbara' AA upgrade and fitting of turret started, upgrade was not completed.
1944–1945: *Z25*, *Z28*, *Z29*, *Z30* searchlight on after funnel replaced with FuMO 63; *Z25* fitted with additional FuMO 63 on foremast; spray strake forward. *Z28* one additional quad 20mm fitted on after deckhouse roof and two single 37mm abaft No 2 mount; *Z28*, *Z29* FuMO 21 replaced with FuMO 24/25; *Z30* removal of catwalks over torpedo tubes; *Z30* fitted with one quad 20mm on after deckhouse and one quad 20mm in front of bridge.

AA fits at end of war:

Z25 – Two twin 37mm on deckhouse behind turret, two twin and two single 37mm on AA deck, two single 37mm abreast the former No 3 gun. Two twin 20mm on forecastle aft of turret, two twin 20mm in bridge wings, two quad 20mm in place of No 2 gun, one single 20mm at the bow. The 37mm were the new Flak M42 mounts.

Z28 – Two twin 37mm on AA deck, two single 37mm on deckhouse behind No 2 gun. One single 20mm at the bow, two single 20mm on AA deck, two quad 20mm on roof of after deckhouse.

Z29 – Two single 55mm in place of twin 37mm on AA deck. Two twin 37mm on AA deck in place of single 20mm, one single 37mm in place of No 2 gun, two single 37mm abreast the former No 2 gun. One twin 20mm on forecastle, two quad 20mm in front of bridge, two twin 20mm in bridge wings, one quad 20mm in place of No 2 gun, one twin 20mm on quarterdeck.

Z30 – Two twin 37mm on AA deck. One quad 20mm in front of bridge, two 20mm singles on AA deck, one quad 20mm atop after deckhouse, one single 20mm under the barrel of No 3 gun.

Notes: The type displayed improved stability qualities and the minimum fuel level was reduced to 10 per cent.

They still rolled heavily due to the weight of armament carried up high; when fitted with the twin turret they suffered badly from reduced buoyancy forward and were subject to speed restrictions to avoid damage in heavy seas. Never fitted with the turret, *Z28* was more seaworthy than her sisters.

This class was popularly known as the 'Narviks', in honour of the ships lost there in April 1940. Naming of the ships was dropped in favour of the First World War practice of only giving numbers to ships below light cruiser size.

Type 1936A (Mob) (*Z31–Z34*, *Z37–Z39*)
General Characteristics: This class was a repeat of the Type 1936A with a few minor differences. The leading edge of the forward funnel cap was curved and the outboard

Z25 in Norwegian waters still fitted with her forward single 5.9in gun. Life rafts are fitted to the side of each gun mount and against the bridge wings. The foremast is either dark grey or black.

edges of the bridge wings were squared off.

AA Fit: two twin 37mm mounts on the AA deck; one quad 20mm atop the after deckhouse and six single 20mm (one at the bow, one forward of the bridge atop the deckhouse, two on the AA deck, one under the barrel of No 3 mount, and one under the barrel of No 4 mount).

Boats: One cutter on davits to port on the forecastle beside the forward funnel; the derrick forward was not fitted – some of the ships did not carry this boat. One motor boat to starboard on the forecastle beside the forward funnel with a derrick fitted just forward. Several of the ships carried cutters to port or starboard under the AA deck.

Individual Differences:

Z31 completed with a single 5.9in forward.

Z31–Z34 had shorter legs to the tripod foremast than *Z37–Z39.*

Z38 and *Z39* were completed with a 20mm quad atop the forward deckhouse instead of a single.

Z39 was fitted with a combined spray strake/degaussing cable that circled the hull at main deck level; the rest had degaussing cables along the top of the hull.

Z39 carried the Greek royal coat of arms on the sides of the 15cm turret.

Identification Features: Short wide funnels, mainmast atop after deckhouse, small propeller guards halfway up the hull, port side davits and starboard side derrick on forecastle, single mount forward (turret or single gun), curved forward funnel cap, and squared off bridge wings.

MODIFICATIONS

1942–1943: *Z31, Z32* fitted with weather shields on the torpedo tubes.

1943–1944: *Z37, Z38* fitted with a spray strake forward; all but *Z31* fitted with one quad 20mm forward of bridge and twin 20mm in bridge wings.

Jun 1944: *Z32* fitted with two single 37mm in place of 20mm singles on AA deck, after searchlight removed.

Aug 1944: *Z31* fitted with twin turret, and one quad 20mm forward of bridge, FuMO 21 replaced with FuMO 24/25.

1944: *Z33, Z39* fitted with weather shields on the torpedo tubes.

1944–1945: *Z31, Z33, Z34* searchlight on after funnel replaced with FuMO 63; *Z31* fitted with FuMO 231 Euklid AA radar and FuMB Metox, fitted with four twin 37mm forward of the bridge, two single 37mm in place of 20mm singles on AA deck, infrared detection gear in the bridge wings; *Z33, Z34* FuMO 21 replaced with FuMO 24/25; *Z33* fitted with FuMB 31, FuMB 4 Sumatra, FuMB 6 Palau, FuMZ 6 and FuMB 3 Bali, FuMB 26 Tunis fitted at masthead; *Z34* fitted with FuMB 34.

Feb 1945: *Z31* fitted with single 4.1in gun forward after action damage.

Apr 1945: *Z39* 'Barbara' AA upgrade completed, searchlight on after funnel replaced with FuMO 63, four FuMB 4 Sumatra aerials fitted to foremast searchlight platform, FuMB 3 Bali and FuMO 81 Berlin S at the masthead.

May 1945: *Z33* No 2 gun landed and fitted to *Z34. Z33* fitted with two twin 37mm ahead of bridge, two twin 37mm on AA deck, two single 37mm on AA deck, one twin 37mm in place of No 2 gun and two twin 20mm in bridge wings; some of the guns came from the sunken *Lützow. Z34* fitted with No 2 gun from *Z33* in place of damaged mounting; *Z34* fitted with one and possibly three single 40mm in front of bridge, two single 37mm in place of 20mm singles on AA deck, and RAG anti-aircraft rockets.

AA fits at end of war:

Z31 – Four twin 37mm forward of the

Z34 in 1943. The degaussing cable is quite evident in this view. The starboard side forecastle derrick is an identification feature for the Type 1936A (Mob). She has been fitted with a quad 20mm in front of the bridge; funnel cowls are silver.

Z39 in drydock on 13 August 1945 shortly after her arrival in the USA. The complex shape of the stern can be seen as well as how the mine rails extended outboard over the stern. There is a pile of three life rafts abaft No 3 gun which has had its barrel cut off. (*US National Archives NH 75378*)

bridge, two twin and two single 37mm on AA deck. Two twin 20mm on forecastle, two twin 20mm in bridge wings, one quad 20mm on after deckhouse.
Z39 – Two twin 37mm on deckhouse behind turret, two twin and two single 37mm on AA deck, two twin 37mm abreast the former No 2 gun. Two twin 20mm in bridge wings, two quad 20mm in place of No 2 gun.

Notes: The (Mob) in their designation is short for *Mobilisierung* (Mobilisation), suggesting that this class was ordered under the same type of emergency wartime program as the British War Emergency destroyers. Not surprisingly, they suffered from the same sea-keeping problems as the Type 1936A. At 3600 tons fully loaded, they were the largest destroyers to see service in the Second World War.

Type 1936B (Mob) (*Z35–Z36, Z43–Z45*)
General Characteristics: This class was a repeat of the Type 1936A with a reversion to five single 5in main guns with the same layout as the Type 1934, reflecting the overloading caused by the heaver 5.9in armament on the Type 1936A. They all completed with FuMO 24/25 and only *Z35* carried a searchlight. The mainmast was stepped in front of No 3 mount, the AA deck was reshaped with the cut-out on the starboard side removed, and all were fitted with weather shields on the torpedo tubes.

AA Fit: Two twin 37mm on the AA deck; three quad 20mm (two on sponsons abreast the bridge radar office, one atop the after deckhouse), two twin 20mm on the AA deck.

Boats: One motor boat on davits to port on the forecastle beside the forward funnel. One cutter on davits to starboard on the forecastle beside the forward funnel. No heavy derricks were fitted. One cutter on davits fitted to port partially under the AA deck.

Individual Differences:
Z43 had a spray strake/degaussing cable at the main deck level from just aft of the anchors to the stern; the others had the degaussing cable along the top of the hull.
Z35 had a searchlight on the foremast
Z43 had a springing jaguar emblem on the sides of the bridge.

Identification Features: Short wide funnels, two gun mounts forward, mainmast in front of No 3 gun, small propeller guards halfway up the hull, quad 20mm on bridge.

MODIFICATIONS
No known upgrades. *Z35* No 3 gun was without a barrel after October 1944 due to a gun mount explosion.

Notes: *Z44* and *Z45* were both launched in 1944 but never completed. *Z44* was hit by bombs while being fitted out in July 1944 and sank in Bremen harbour. Her wreck and the uncompleted *Z45* were cannibalized for parts for repairs to *Z39*.

Due to the combination of the large hull and lighter main armament, this class was actually the best destroyer design produced by the Kriegsmarine. By the time they were completed, their theatre of operations was confined to the Baltic so there was no opportunity to show their capabilities on the open ocean.

Z1 Leberecht Maass (Type 1934), 1937

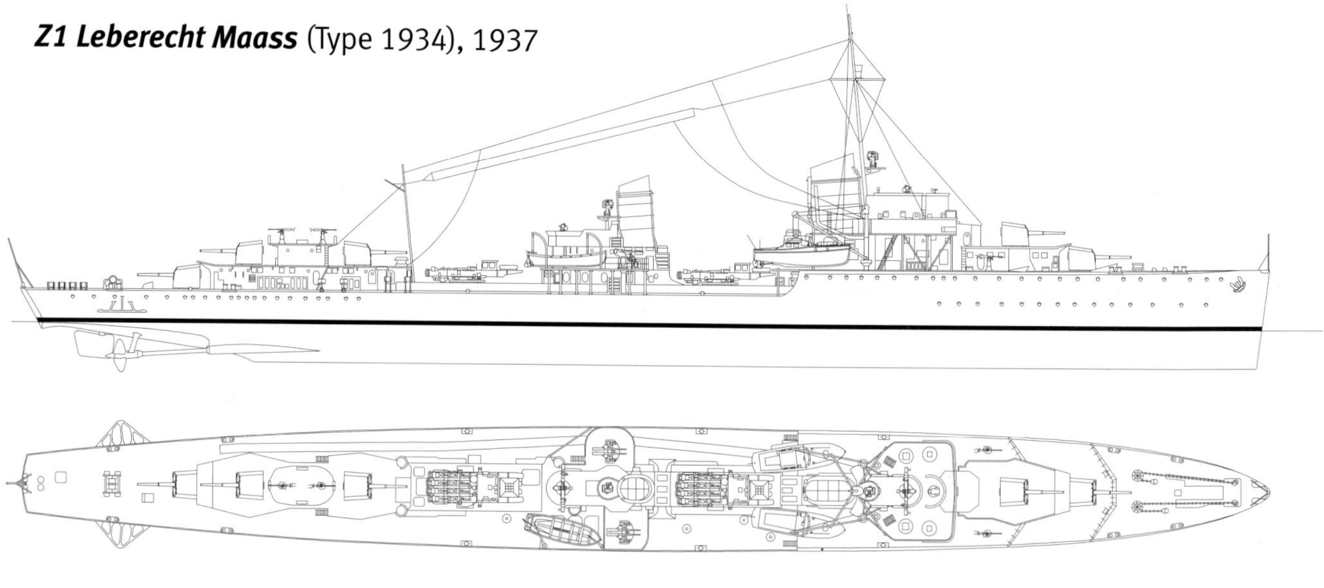

Z2 Georg Thiele (Type 1934), 1938

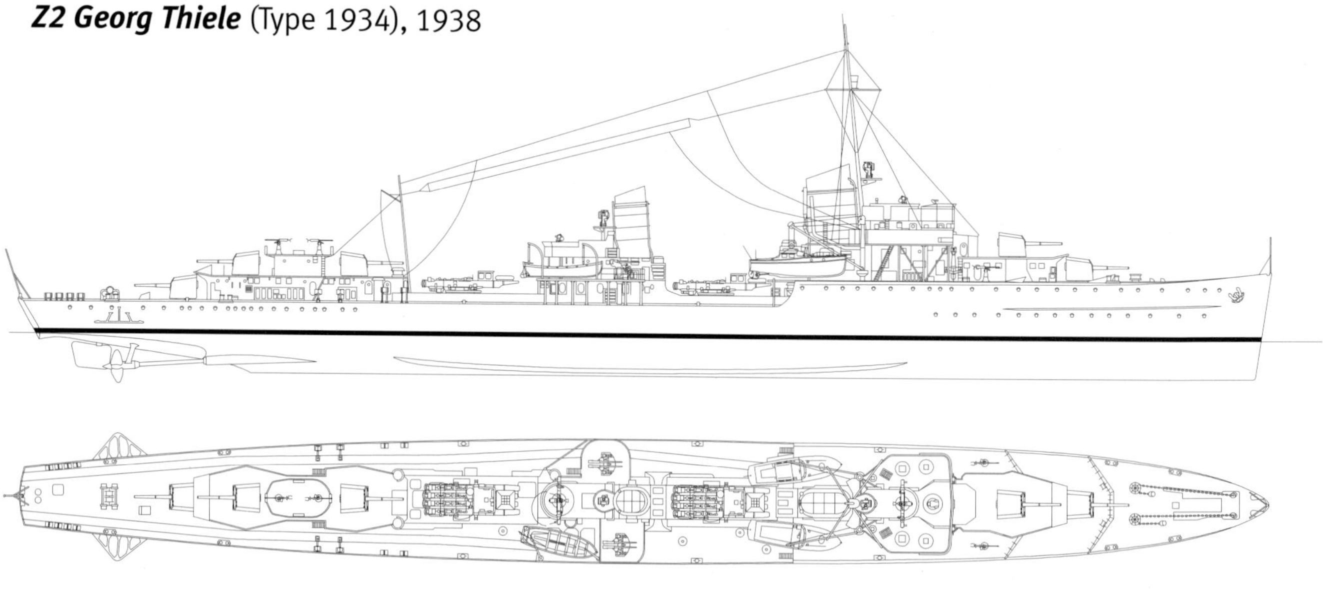

Z5 Paul Jacobi (Type 1934A), 1943

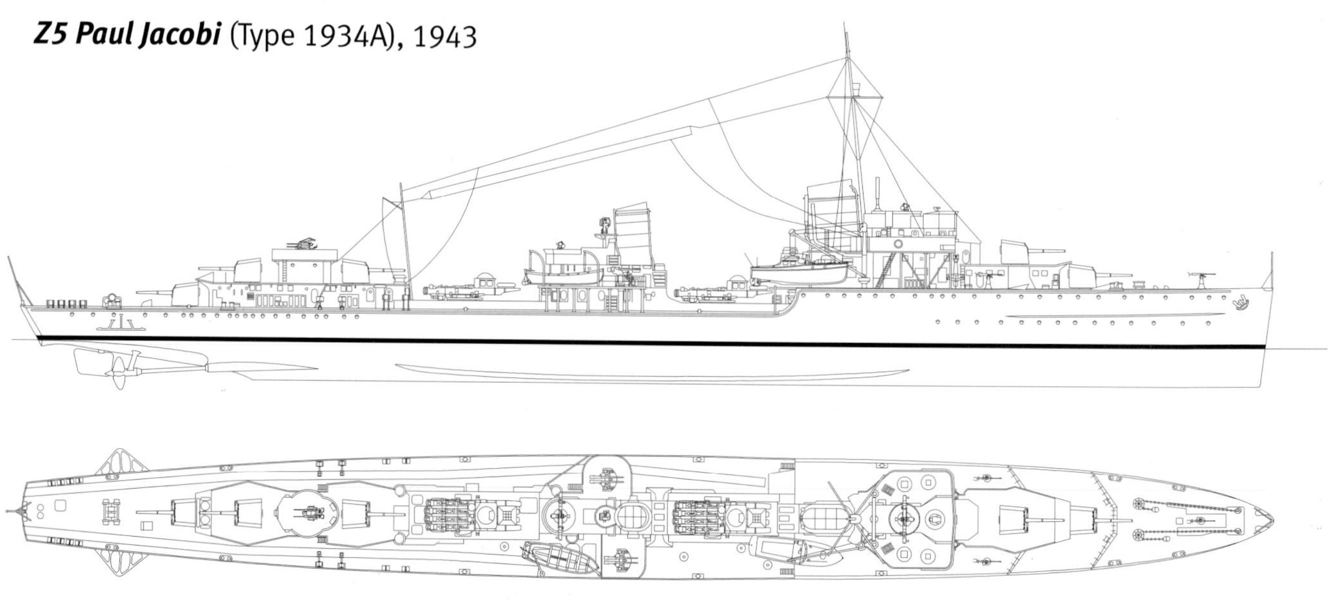

Z5 Paul Jacobi (Type 1934A), 1945

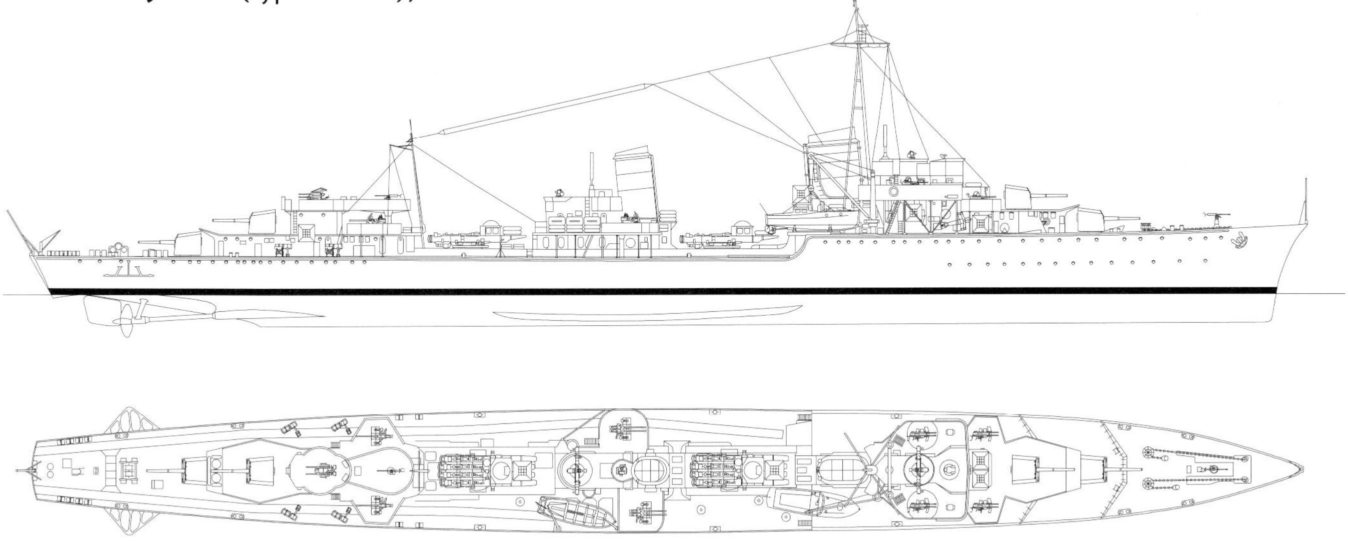

Z20 Karl Galster (Type 1936), 1942

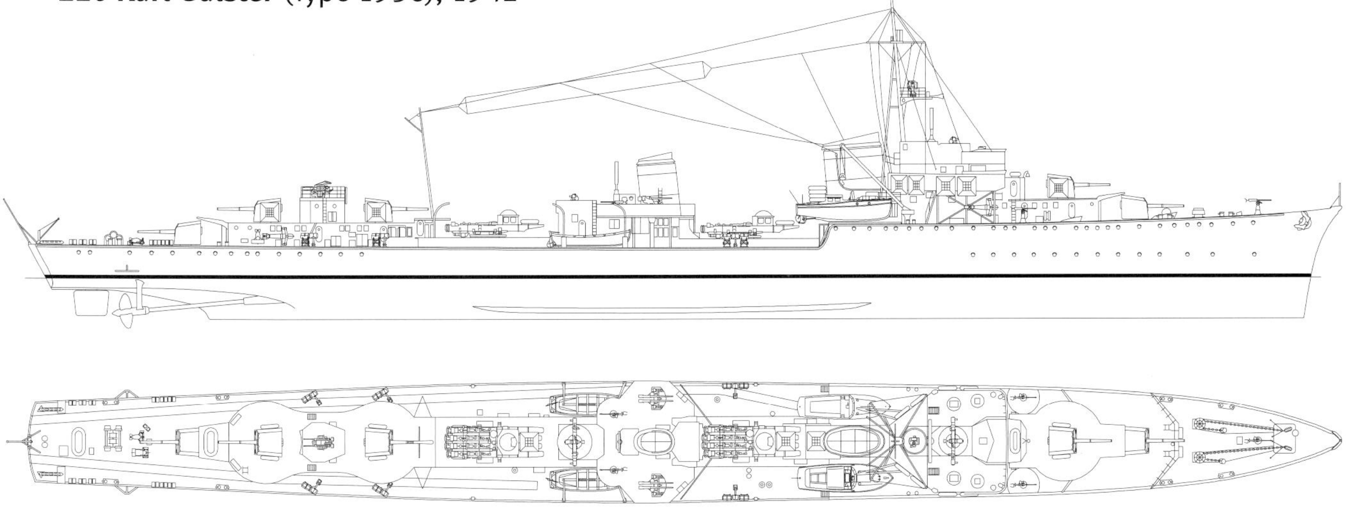

Z23 (Type 1936A), 1940

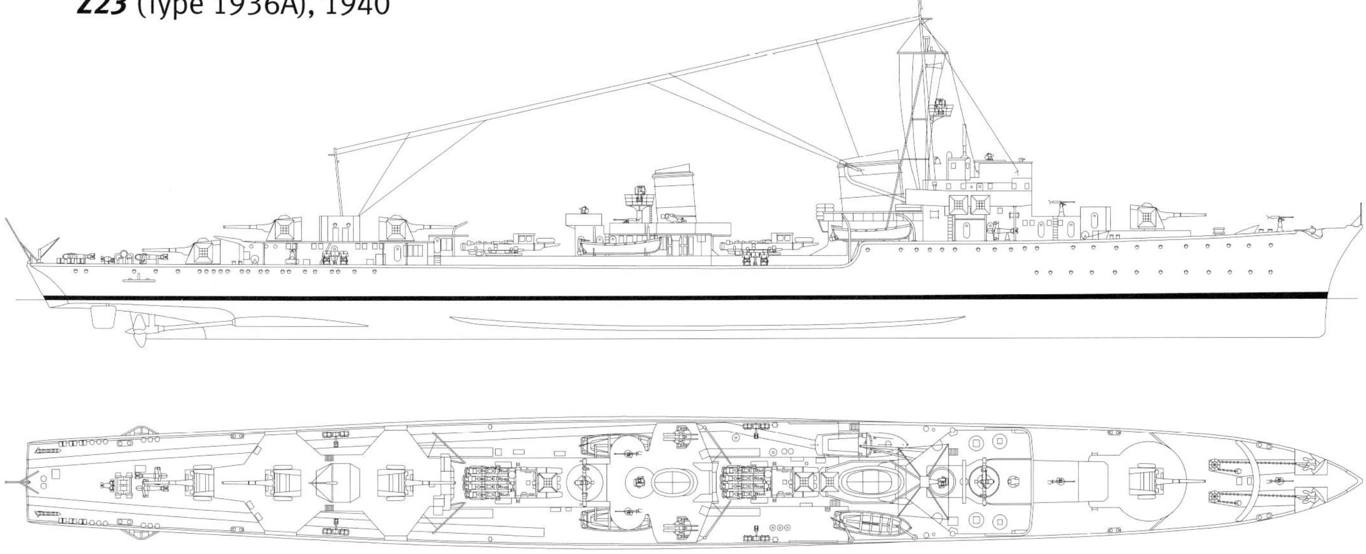

Z25 (Type 1936A), 1944

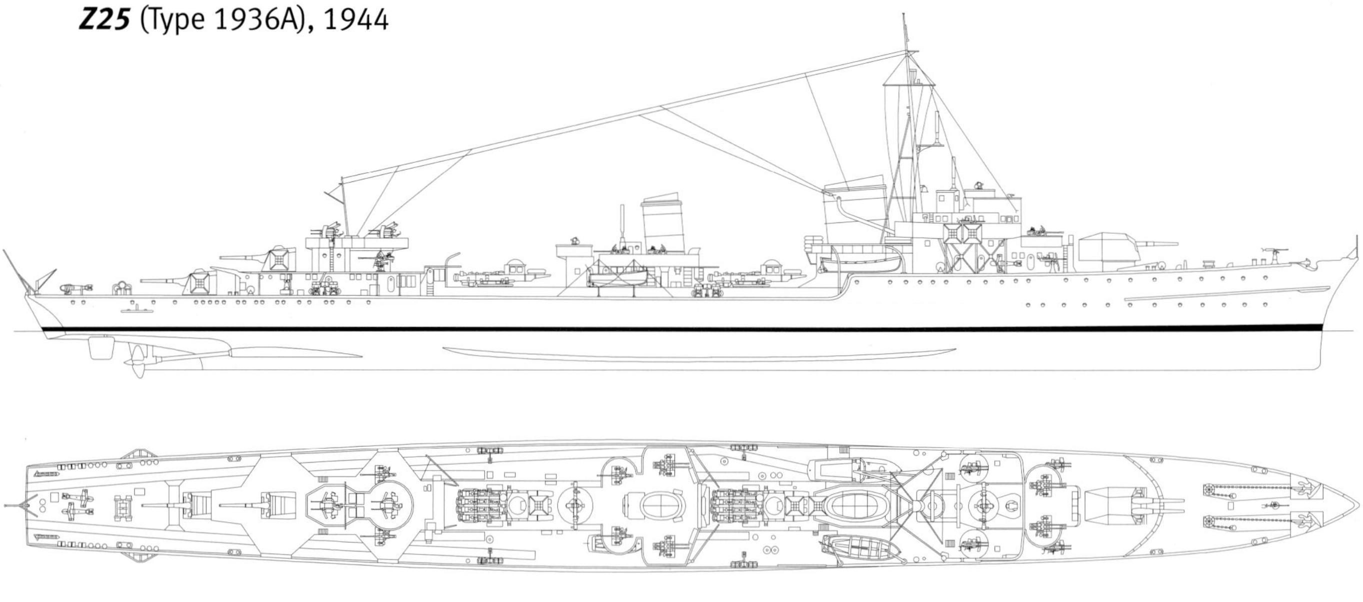

Z28 (Type 1936A), 1942

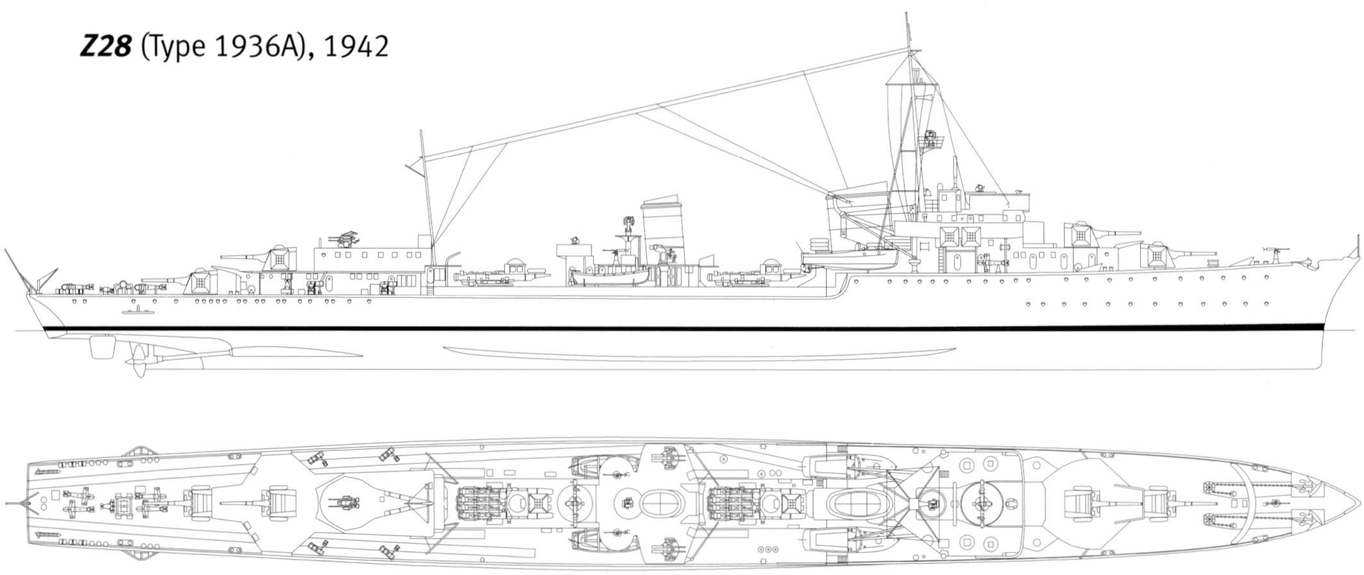

Z28 (Type 1936A), 1945

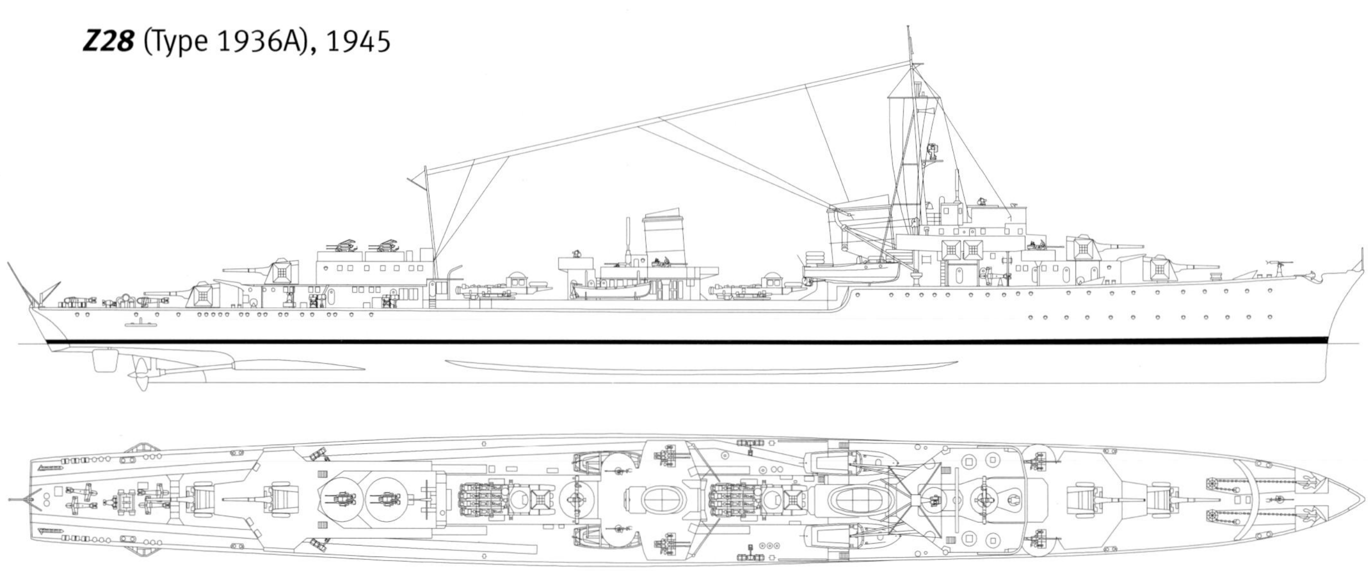

Z31 (Type 1936A Mob), 1945

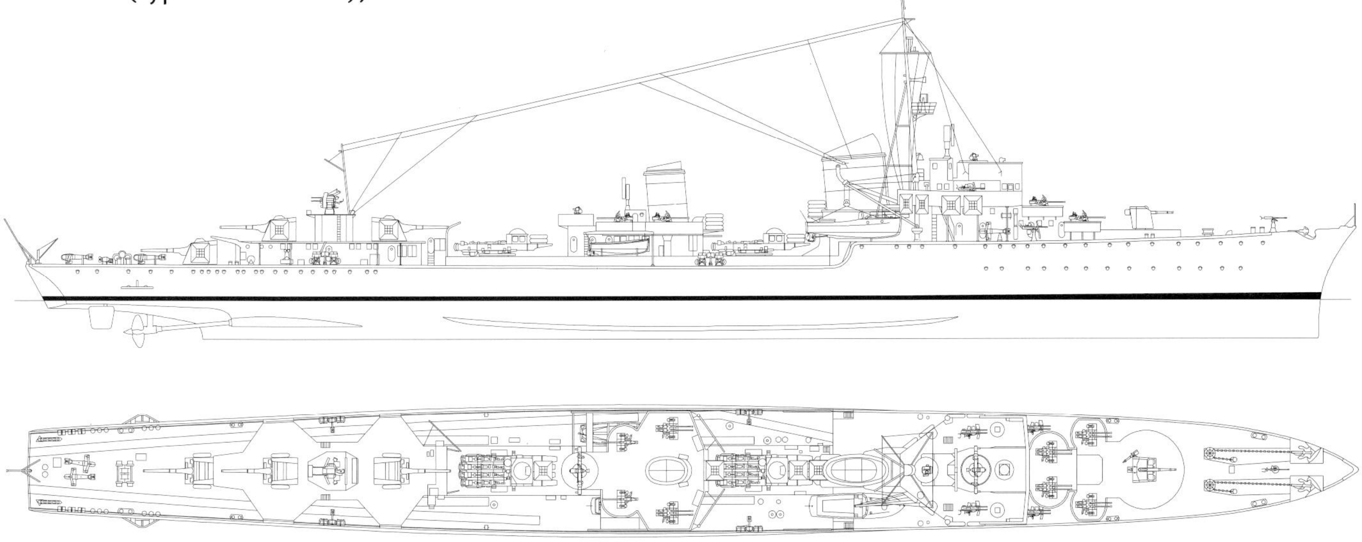

Z32 (Type 1936A Mob), 1942

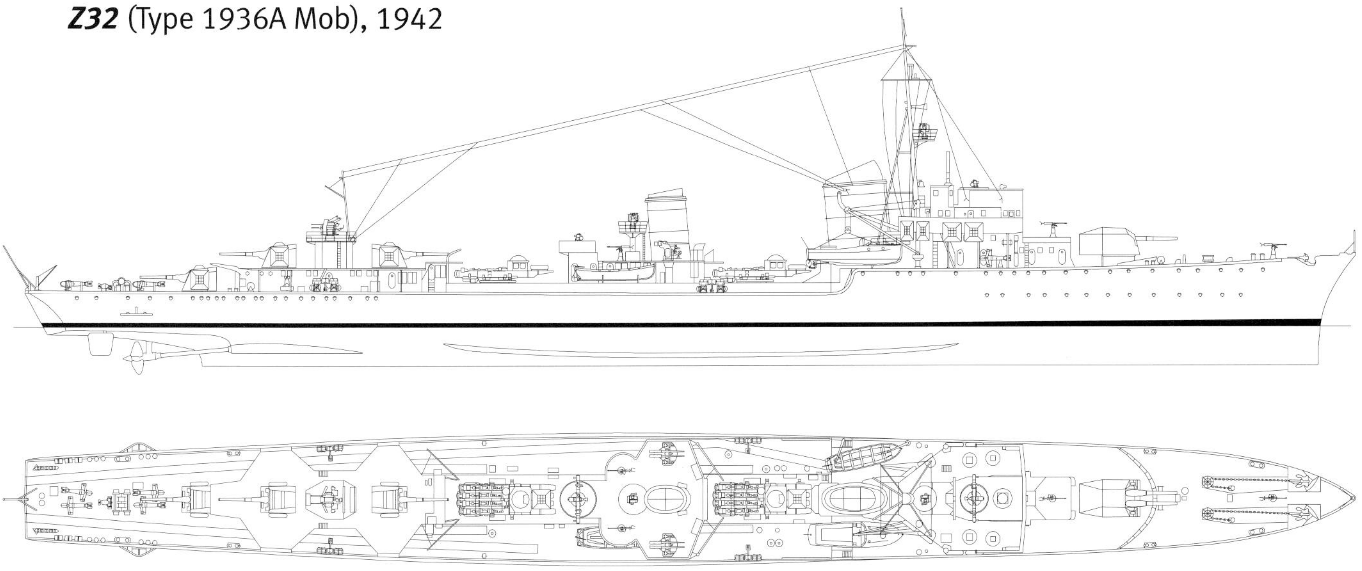

Z43 (Type 1936B Mob), 1944

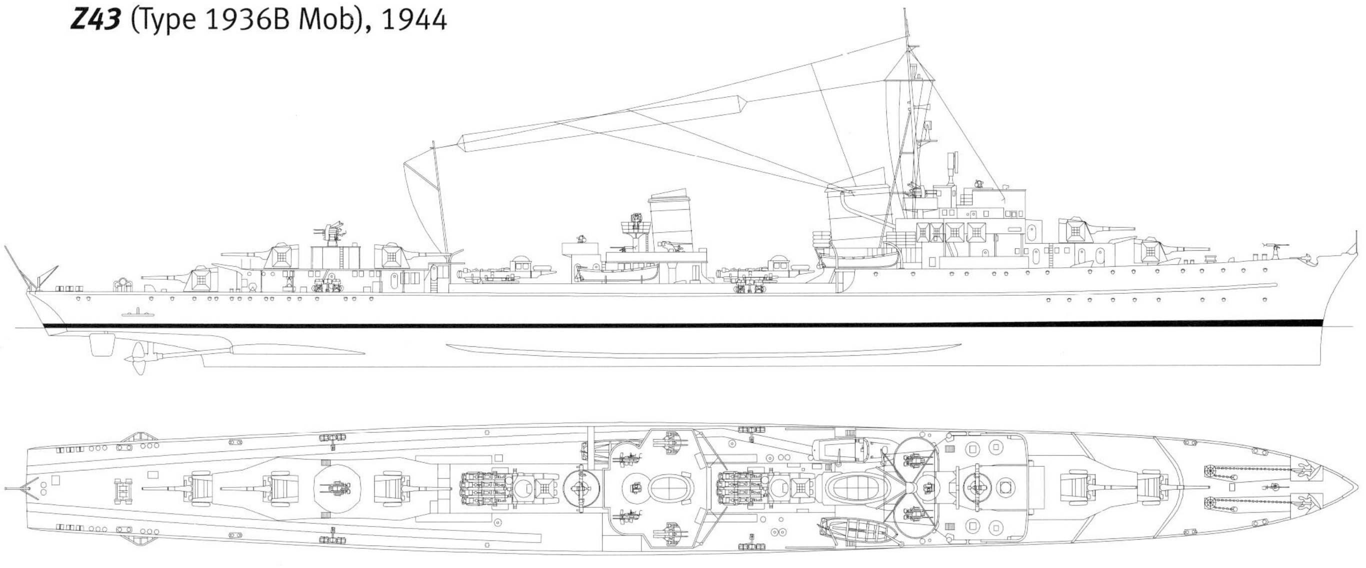

Selected References

BIBLIOGRAPHY

Asmussen, John and Leon, Eric, *German Naval Camouflage Volume One 1939–1941* (Seaforth & Naval Institute Press 2012). The first volume of an extensive study of German warship camouflage with many colour drawings and photographs.

Leon, Eric and Asmussen, John, *German Naval Camouflage Volume Two 1942–1945* (Seaforth & Naval Institute Press 2014). The second volume of the authors' extensive study of German warship camouflage with many colour drawings and photographs. This volume contains many more drawings of the destroyers than the first volume.

Beaver, Paul, *German Destroyers and Escorts* (AZTEX Corporation 1981). A picture album of the Kriegsmarine destroyers and torpedo boats; many interesting and unique photos

Bekker, Cajus, *Hitler's Naval War* (Doubleday 1974). An operational history of the German Navy in World War II with excellent analyses of the German Naval High Command and its shortcomings.

Brown, D K, RCNC, 'Post War Trials Tests against Destroyers', *Warship XI* (Conway Maritime Press & Naval Institute Press 1987). A discussion of the background to the explosive tests with notes about the effect to each ship tested.

Hervieux, Pierre, 'German Destroyer Minelaying Operations off the English Coast (1940–41)', *Warship IV* (Conway Maritime Press 1980). A detailed article about each of the minelaying operations, with good background information and a list of victims.

Jacobsen, Alf R., *Death At Dawn* (The History Press 2016). A very good account of the political and military background that led to the Norwegian campaign, with a very detailed account of the invasion of Narvik and the First Battle of Narvik.

Koop, Gerhard and Schmolke Klaus-Peter, *German Destroyers of World War II*, (Greenhill Books 2003). A comprehensive look at all the German destroyer classes, with a detailed wartime service section for each ship; many drawings and photographs.

Le Fleming, H M, *Warships of World War I*, (Ian Allen 1970). A comprehensive handbook with details of every Royal Navy and Imperial German Navy vessel that served in World War I; many data tables, photos and line drawings. Invaluable for details of the German torpedo boats and destroyers.

Preston, Antony, 'The Narvik Flotilla: German Destroyer Design 1936-45', *Warship I* (Conway Maritime Press 1977). A three-part article about the Type 1936A, Type 1936A (Mob), and Type 1936B (Mob) classes with their technical background, class details, and wartime careers; many drawings.

Preston, Antony, *Super Destroyers* (Conway Maritime Press 1978). A look at the big destroyers built in the 1930s by Britain, France, German, Italy, Japan and the USA. The section on the German destroyers is a repeat of the information in *Warship I* but with fewer drawings.

Sieche, Erwin, 'German Naval Radar to 1945', *Warship VI* (Conway Maritime Press 1982). A two-part article about German naval radar with technical information and many drawings.

Whitley, M J, *Destroyer! – German Destroyers in World War II* (Arms and Armour Press 1983). A thorough look at the design, construction, and operational history of German destroyers and torpedo boats.

Whitley, M J, *Destroyers of World War Two – An International Encyclopedia* (Arms and Armour Press 2000). An extensive study of all the world's destroyers that saw service in World War Two. Many photos and detailed service histories.

INTERNET REFERENCES

German Naval Weapons: http://www.navweaps.com/Weapons/WNGER_Main.php